THE NEW
INDUSTRIAL LANDSCAPE

Overleaf: Erecting the all-welded diesel locomotive plant for the Electro-Motive Corporation, La Grange, Illinois, 1935.

Martin Greif

THE NEW INDUSTRIAL LANDSCAPE

THE STORY OF
THE AUSTIN COMPANY

The Main Street Press   Clinton, New Jersey

Published in the United States of America in 1978 by
The Main Street Press
42 Main Street
Clinton, New Jersey 08809

© 1978 by The Austin Company

All rights reserved. No part of this publication may be
reproduced, stored in a retrieval system, or transmitted, in
any form or by any means, electronic, mechanical, photocopying,
recording, or otherwise, without the prior permission
of the publisher.

Library of Congress Catalog Card Number: 77–87118
ISBN 0–87663–308–4

Printed in the United States of America
by Pearl-Pressman Liberty/Printers

Designed by Quentin Fiore

And I have filled him with the spirit of God, in wisdom, and in understanding, and in knowledge, and in all manner of workmanship. . . .

Exodus 31:3

The description of Bezaleel, the first builder-engineer.

Contents

Preface   9

The New Industrial Landscape   13

The Story of The Austin Company   25
- I   The Founding   25
- II   Speed and Standardization   55
- III The New Era: Austin in the '30s   93
- IV   Austin Goes to War   129
- V   An International Organization   143
- VI   The Second Hundred Years   181

Index   189

Preface

Four years ago, while working on a book about American design during the Great Depression, I discovered The Austin Company in the same way that many people have over the past half century. I came upon an Austin advertisement in *Fortune* magazine and soon sought out others. What I saw in those faded, dog-eared pages of the 1930s were models of buildings so advanced for their time—and yet so fundamentally American in scale and in design—that they were completely unlike any others pictured in that conservative business magazine. If these structures still possessed the power to startle forty years after their inception, what must have been their impact in their own day? Eventually, when my book was published, I suggested to its readers, many of whom were young enough to be discovering the '30s for the first time, that the work of The Austin Company advanced the cause of modern design in America as much as did the work of the period's great architects: Lescaze, Harrison, Kahn, Keck, and Stone. I did not then suspect that I would be invited to write an entire book about The Austin Company.

That I bring to the present book a bias favorably disposed to the subject is obvious. Far less evident, however, are the terms under which I agreed to undertake this project, terms which I think go a long way towards an understanding of this most unusual corporate organization.

The Austin Company is celebrating its centennial at a time in which the writing of corporate histories is highly suspect, and correctly so. *The Wall Street Journal* and other business periodicals have criticized many such books as worthless, as "ego trips for the company's chief executive and current top management." Or, as one reporter has recently noted, corporate histories frequently "paint the corporation as a center of sanctity in a sinful world—like a fortress monastery in the Dark Ages preserving virtue against the onslaughts of barbarians; I doubt that anybody has ever swallowed that kind of bilge."

From the outset, and long before I was invited to undertake this history, the management of The Austin Company was sensitive to "that kind of bilge" and wanted no part of it. What it did want, however, was an objective *book* and not a public relations pamphlet. There was, as well, unanimous agreement that any book worthy of the company had to be written by an outsider who could bring an independent point of view to the subject.

If one is to believe the reports in *The Wall Street Journal* about the horrors that writers face in compiling company histories, then I have been blessed. No one has attempted to persuade me to adopt any view of events other than my own. Nor has anything been hidden from me. I have had complete access to all extant documents and records. Even the few skeletons rattling in the corporate transfiles have been cheerfully exposed to light, as have transcripts of litigations over the years and the complete minutes of board meetings. I have been encouraged to seek out as many employees—both present and past—as I had need and time to interview.

Austin management has allowed me, too, to select a format for the book that is consistent with my analysis of the existing records. Understandably, Samuel Austin and his early colleagues were far too busy practicing their trade and building their company to greatness to have been mindful of what history might possibly think of them a century later. Consequently, the Austin archives are far from complete, the most notable loss, perhaps, being the absence of any written records that might have been kept by the company's first three presidents. The archives, however, are extraordinarily rich in photographs that almost completely document the company's work in the twentieth century, a richness that suggests that Austin's history might very well be written in terms of its buildings rather than in a detailed analysis of its personnel.

The New Industrial Landscape, then, is somewhat different in format from the usual company biography. It is a heavily illustrated book in which buildings loom larger than men. And this, I think, is as it should be. The business of Austin, after all, is building. And its motto, "Results, Not Excuses," clearly dictates that the Results to be emphasized, to be studied, are constructed of brick and lime and glass and steel. Their very excellence, one need hardly add, is a constant reminder that they were wrought by flesh and blood—in short, by men.

I gratefully acknowledge the cooperation of the management of The Austin Company in the compilation of this book. Their disdain of puffery, reflecting an unwavering confidence in the integrity of their company, is best summarized by the simple advice given me at the outset of the project by Charles A. Shirk, president of The Austin Company: "Whatever else you do, just tell the truth."

The following people have helped me do just that: Allan S. Austin, Donald G. Austin, Margaret Austin Rodgers; Harold A. Anderson, Hamilton Beatty, Paul Eden, Rollin R. Eiber, Wallace R. Engstrom, David H. Kempler, Albert S. Low, A. H. Meyer, A. T. Waidelich; and members of the present corporate staff: T. J. Judge, T. B. Sweeney, C. B. Utley, A. A. Wilhelm. The many members of the staff who have helped me see the company through their eyes, but are too numerous to mention individually, have already received my thanks.

Throughout, I have enjoyed the invaluable assistance of H. E. B. Anderson—no visitor to foreign shores could ever have had a better guide—and the fine counsel of Marvin M. Epstein. Finally, I acknowledge the contribution of B. R. Sayer, who—inadvertently, perhaps—taught me one reason for The Austin Company's greatness: its directors and managers are engineers or architects first; executives, second.

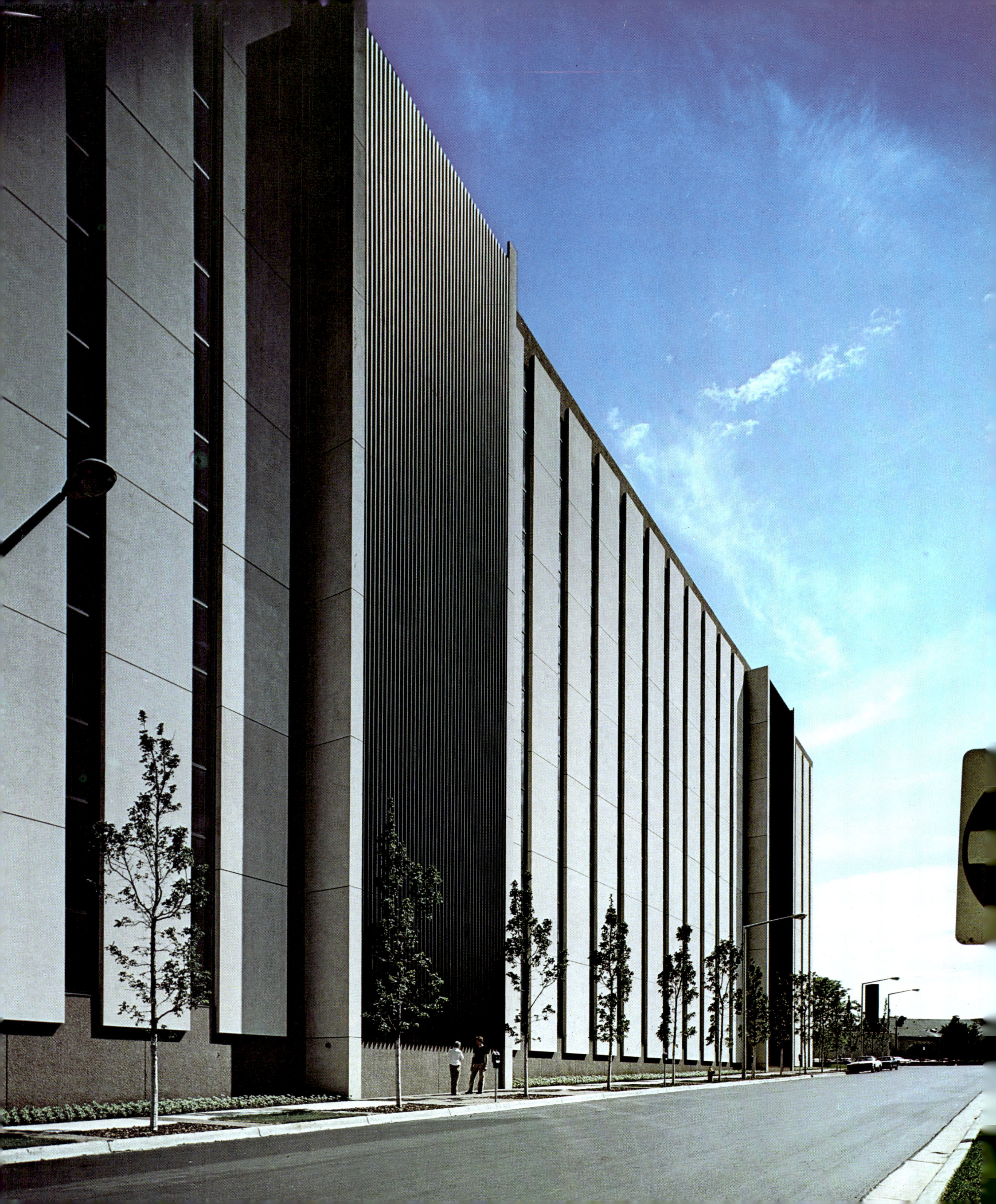

The New Industrial Landscape

1

The building sits massively beneath a blue northwestern sky, solid, vast, and mute, a block of white illumined by the sun. Surrounded by a forest of evergreens, the verdant scrub indigenous to a craggy landscape that slopes gradually to a quiet fishing village below and towards Puget Sound beyond, it rises monolithically from its setting, its presence a paradox not easily resolved. It seems at once an alien intruder, a mammoth cube of steel and concrete left within the woods by a race of giants. But it is, as well, so perfectly proportioned, so precisely sited and designed, that it might have sprung with nature from the very earth on which it lies.

The structure is enormous, a colossus that surely would have stirred the imaginations of the ancients. But just how large it is eludes the naked eye. Set amidst a complexity of buildings, private roads, and neatly landscaped parking lots—the whole bordered on three sides by dense thickets of hemlock, spruce, and pine—there is little from which to gain a knowing sense of scale. At first glance it seems oddly smaller than it really is, its exceptional length truncating its height in an illusion of diminished space. But a distant moving vehicle, dwarfed on the horizon where it glides along the building's side, remains minuscule as it reaches the foreground, a speck grown into a dot. The viewer is suddenly overwhelmed: his eye can in no way take the total structure in at once. It might as well be a skyscraper lying on its side.

Large and imposing as it is, it is not easily thought of as handsome. Neither is it ugly. It is, instead, neutral, even stately in its functional plainness—very much like a parcel before it is wrapped, a gift box without its fancy decoration, but insistently intriguing nonetheless, inviting one to peer beyond the surface to discover the promise of the contents deep within.

There is little here, consequently, to attract the architectural critic whose view of building is from the outside in, and whose concerns extend but rarely to what lies beneath the skin. Those who love mere surfaces have rarely learned to open doors.

But beyond these walls, beyond the surface and within the concrete box itself, lies a complexity of movement that can be likened to the active rhythms of a city deep in motion. Beyond the surface lies a space so vast that men and women move about

Research and Development Center, The Upjohn Company, Kalamazoo, Michigan, 1970.

on bicycles or in electric cars, propelled through corridors that lead like major roads to cities smaller still within the expansive plain. The building is alive with the craft of engineering made visible: Trusses and columns, power lines, sprinkler pipes and outlets, duct work and ventilators are all exposed. Nothing structural is hidden, nothing camouflaged. The eye widens to absorb a panoply of brilliant color, patterns emerging in swift succession to rival the ineluctable logic of modern art. Color everywhere. Color within a man-made world that only gradually is seen to be without windows, an abstraction of blues and yellows and reds of every shade and nuance. Here one color consistently defines the stairwells; there another marks electrical ducts and conduits; and still another, the shafts of pipe for air conditioning. Instead of hiding and obscuring, color here becomes an agent charged with emphasizing and revealing—and becomes as well the handmaiden of safety, defining areas of work, demarking apparatus and locations, and indicating flow of traffic. The total effect against so huge a panorama is breathtaking—beauty that soars beyond the rainbow, frozen not on canvas but in steel.

From a catwalk almost 115 feet above the main floor one turns and views the quadrants of a vast area below: almost a million and a half square feet—and this a fraction of the structure's total volume: more than 200 million cubic feet of open space. From this vantage point, amidst a skeleton of steel as intricate in its graceful strength as that of Paxton was a century before, time seems almost to stand still. The movement subjacent is barely perceptible, though audible. And yet there *is* motion. An object below, glistening with the glyptic grace of an enormous Brancusi, is gradually coming into being.

There is activity indeed. But the vastness of the room engulfs the immense object below, just as the object itself dwarfs in turn the human workers who move like Liliputians before the outstretched form of some metallic Gulliver. In the same thirty days in which a million cans or jars or tubes will speed within the automated machinery of a modern factory, only eight of the objects glistening below can inch their way to consummation, but so slowly that the human eye cannot record their movement. Thus time within this capacious space progresses in slow motion. From the catwalk above, Einstein and relativity make perfect sense.

To build this structural behemoth necessitated the labor of 3,500 men. To build it meant moving 6 million cubic yards of earth, almost twice as much earth as was moved in building the Grand Coulee Dam—or enough to build a dyke 12 feet wide and 12 feet high from New York to Washington, D. C. To construct it required as well the erection of a railroad 3 miles long, a spur so steeply graded over rough and raw terrain that it remains the second steepest standard-gauge railroad in the United States. In addition, 515 acres of ground were leveled and filled; 135 acres of 4-inch thick asphalt were laid; a 15 million gallon retention basin was dug; 200,000 cubic yards of concrete were poured; and 43,000 tons of structural steel were put up and held together with over 420,000 high-strength bolts. So immense is this extraordinary building that, if all the steel for its construction had been shipped at once, a train more than 15 miles long would have been required.

For this is a structure in which almost five million separate parts are assembled to build an airplane so large that the Wright Brothers' first flight at Kitty Hawk could have been performed within the length of its fuselage alone. This is the Boeing 747 plant, one of the engineering marvels of the twentieth century, an age in which the ability to marvel has been all but lost. Now a decade old, it is only one of many thousands of structures designed and built by The Austin Company during the past one-hundred years. Measured on a scale of construction time per cubic foot, it is the fastest-built industrial structure in the world.

It is, in fact, the largest structure ever built by man.

2

The birth of Samuel Austin, founder of the company that bears his name, occurred at just that moment in history in which a radical technological revolution was taking place that would in time alter not only his life and that of his contemporaries, but that of all future generations as well. For the birth of Samuel Austin and the birth of the modern industrial age both occurred at about the same time and in the same place: in England in the middle of the nineteenth century.

The story of The Austin Company, consequently, is best understood against the background of a rapidly changing technology that in a matter of mere decades succeeded in shrinking the size of continents and oceans and in opening the vast possibilities of the stars beyond—as well as planting the twin seeds of twentieth-century promise and despair: the development of human potentiality and the overhanging threat of universal self-destruction.

The history of modern technology and the history of The Austin Company run parallel courses. One reason, in fact, why Austin has successfully survived a century of competition in a business noted for its notoriously short lifespan and high mortality is its conscientious awareness of the vicissitudes of just this fact. In almost every stage of its history, The Austin Company has acted on a keen understanding of the most recent technological knowledge. Like a mirror, it has in its hundred years of building reflected every major engineering innovation. And, just as frequently, it has contributed to that same technology advances of its own. The company that Samuel Austin founded, therefore, witnessed every development of the new industrial age. More than that, it was an active participant in a technological revolution that changed the very course of daily life: It designed and built structures that, more than being mere shelters, became the very means of production itself. And in building structures that provided the essential goods and services on which modern man depends, it created nothing less than a radically new industrial landscape.

The birth of the modern industrial age in the middle of the nineteenth century coincided with the discovery of iron to be used for machinery and transport. Iron and industry—material *for* machinery and production *by* machinery—are implicit in each other. Their joint conception, namely the conception of "technique," was the symbol of a new age, of a new generation. That first generation of inventors, entrepreneurs, and investors regarded industrialism as more or less their own creation, as some magnificent weapon forged for private use, as something national rather than international, fighting competitors both at home and abroad. In a day that valued the new machinery more than the human beings who operated it, the factories of the nineteenth century were overcrowded, dark, and dreary places that created within the public consciousness a revulsion with industry that has been slow in dying. By the opening of the twentieth century the old industrial landscape of the burgeoning cities was marked by a sharp contrast between the lifeless monotony of its multi-storied factories and the unproductive swagger of its commercial buildings and offices then rising imperially against a suffocating sky.

World War I marked the end of this first stage of development. The economic and social results of that war produced what was the beginning of a fundamental change of attitude, particularly towards the needs of the industrial worker, an attitude anticipated in part by The Austin Company several years earlier. Industrialism began to be regarded in a clearer perspective and the essential principles of its activity to be recognized. Science had previously regarded material and energy as separate from each other. But in the period just prior to the Great War, the two conceptions came gradually to be recognized as merely different conditions of a single primary element. The modern engineer began, therefore, to abandon the old mechanistic theory of dead material and to believe in vitalism as the principle to which he was obliged to render service. Machinery, which until the second decade of the twentieth century had been the ready tool of a dead exploitation, strove to become instead the constructive element in a new and living organism.

This new technological optimism dictated that machinery had been born as a necessary by-product of human development, and at the very moment when the need for it arose. Quickened by a growing demand for the wonders of technological invention —electric light, horseless carriages, telephones—an almost universal belief in the benevolence of scientific progress brought about a new understanding of the essential task of machinery. Neither good nor bad in itself, it existed to satisfy, to coordinate, and to control the mutual relations between population and increased production, between industrialization and increased consumption of human material. In this way machinery came to be regarded both as a symbol of the death of the pre-industrial past and as an element of a new and better life which was certain to emerge in the age of scientific wonder.

As applied to industrial construction, this realization meant that the artificial separation of pure engineering calculation and pure architectural inspiration that had occurred earlier in the nineteenth century was now without roots and was invalid in the new era of industrial and commercial design. But by their fusion, however—a fusion pioneered and promulgated early in the twentieth century by The Austin Company—industrialism was able to free itself from merely materialistic limitations. One practical application of this new philosophy of building science, as we will later see, was the invention of the Austin Method, a radical departure in its day and still debated three-quarters of a century later. By turning its back on antiquated methods, the future course of industrial building was clear: The gloomy and desolate factory of older days was gradually to become, in Erich Mendelsohn's visionary phrase, "a temple of labor, a shrine of creative reality." Thus the tremendous surge in international business that followed World War I brought about a concomitant revolution in industrial construction, a revolution that expressed itself in new convincing architectural forms that transformed the industrial landscape and ushered in the "modern" world. This development, of course, coincided with the revolutionary discovery and gradual perfection of new material for construction, in particular of reinforced concrete and steel.

Structural technique and architectural expression simultaneously achieved a common basis when World War I increased industrial production both quantitatively and qualitatively. For reasons that will emerge in the pages that follow, the company that Samuel Austin had founded on the bedrock of nineteenth-century craftsmanship and simple moral values gained national—even international—prominence in this very period of radical twentieth-century change. Basic to its willingness to experiment and innovate was an inherent understanding of the world-changes going on about it. The Austin Company, for example, early recognized that industry—perhaps under the widespread influence of Frederick Winslow Taylor's theories of Scientific Management—was on its guard against wastage of human labor even as it was attempting to avoid the wastage of material which was inseparable from nineteenth-century methods of construction. Industry, in fact, began to rationalize a man's capacity for work at the same time that it began to rationalize its use of bricks and mortar. Both, they realized, were so much raw material. In consequence, as we shall see, Austin pioneered by developing its series of standard fac-

Westminster College, New Wilmington, Pennsylvania, 1972.

Central Operations Building, First Security Corporation, Salt Lake City, Utah, 1976.

Research and Development Center, The Timken Roller Bearing Company, Canton, Ohio, 1965.

Food Processing Center, Kitchens of Sara Lee, Inc., New Hampton, Iowa, 1971.

High Bay Assembly Building, The Boeing Company, Renton, Washington, 1966.

TDI (toluene diisocyante) Plant, BASF-Wyandotte Corporation, Geismar, Louisiana, 1973.

Marketing and Research Center, Monsanto Company, Bath, Ohio, 1968.

tory buildings, an innovation that rendered building an industrial production—and rendered the craft of building an industry of building. Austin thereby helped eliminate the contradiction between human efficiency and machine work by being among the first to regard both as a law of material and ideal self-preservation. Although The Austin Company was hardly alone in presaging industrial modernism, its subsequent history, fostered by an unflagging confidence in engineering research, contributed substantially to opening the way for a homogeneous twentieth-century architectural form by which the logic of the new emerging materials could be uniformly applied to industry, transport, and building.

Since the products of industry, given the clarity and precision of their shape, presented the most authentic evidence of a new capacity for modern form, industrial building—regarded as architectural production—drew its sustenance from the same soil that gave birth to the forms and shapes of technical production. Industrial construction, therefore, led the way towards a new style of architecture, an evolution over several decades that dramatically changed the international skyline and is visually documented in the pages of this book.

The history of The Austin Company is thus inextricably entwined with that of industrial technology. That it began with the emigration of a young English carpenter to America and eventually progressed well beyond the confines of industry alone—encompassing the design and construction of museums, theaters, airports, schools, hotels, and a bewildering array of architectural and engineering versatility—is beyond dispute. But the Austin story nonetheless documents the development of an industrial technology that transcended the death of the nineteenth century and hoped to bring about a fresh new form of creative culture in the twentieth. That this utopian ideal was hopelessly naïve is debatable. But the idealistic morality and ethics that Samuel Austin nurtured in this same historic period are not. Incorporated within the company he founded, they have survived intact through a century of extraordinary change—perhaps the only unchanging entity in an organization noted for its dynamic innovation and its molding of the new industrial landscape.

That this is not mere idle speculation is the fundamental purpose of the pages that follow.

A conference in the office of Wilbert J. Austin (*second from right*), c. 1913. Samuel Austin *(third from left)* presides at the head of the table.

I The Founding

By a happy accident of history, Samuel Austin and the new age of industrial building were born at the very same moment. On June 16, 1850—significantly, a Sabbath day—a son was born to Mary Austin and her husband Thomas in their one-room rustic stone cottage in the English country village of Orton Waterville. At the same time, in London, some sixty miles south, Sir Joseph Paxton had just designed his Crystal Palace, a masterpiece whose revolutionary framework would begin within the next few months to cast its enduring iron shadow over the destiny of the nineteenth century.

The correspondence between Sir Joseph Paxton and the birth of Samuel Austin goes beyond mere poetic happenstance: The one made possible the new industrial age; the other grew up to found a company that would help to bring it to full flower. And there were similarities of class as well: Both were born in abject rural poverty—the one, a farmer's son; the other, the son of a laborer who could neither read nor write. And—most astonishing of all, given their eventual accomplishments as builders of the modern world—neither received the slightest training as an architect or as an engineer.

The early history of The Austin Company is the history of Samuel Austin himself. For, until he was joined years later by his son, Samuel Austin *was* The Austin Company, a man of energetic perseverance and high moral principle who developed his company's potential strength and ethical ideals as he consistently confirmed his own. The story of these early years has been told several times, but never quite so simply or so well as this fine man once rendered it himself.

Samuel Austin's Autobiography Samuel Austin's autobiographical memoir, delivered informally to a group of employees about eight years after the firm was first incorporated in 1904, deserves to speak for itself. It will be interrupted only occasionally and briefly by editorial glosses whenever they are necessary to make the history more complete:

The Apprenticeship "In the year 1866, I was bound as an apprentice to a Mr. William Rollings of the village of Orton Waterville, county of Huntington, England, to serve as apprentice learning the carpenter, joiner, and building business, Mr. Rollings agreeing to instruct me, or to cause me to be instructed, in the said business, according to the best means in his power. On June 16, 1866, I was sixteen years old and I was bound from that date to June 16, 1871, my twenty-first birthday.

"The compensation I was to receive was to be as follows: the first year, 3 shillings per week; the second year, 4s. per week; the third year, 5s. per week; the fourth year, 6s. per week; and the fifth year 8s. per week. In addition, my father, Thomas Austin, paid £10 to William Rollings as a premium for his teaching me the business."

[In 1866, the year of Samuel Austin's indenture, England was struck by the worst economic panic in its history. That Thomas Austin was able to pay Rollings £10—even though it was due in two installments, the second payable at the end of two years—is nothing short of miraculous and clearly indicates that this good and upright man must have scrimped and saved during his son's youth to provide him with a trade. The terms of the indenture reflect the strict moral environment in which Samuel Austin was raised. During the term of service, the apprentice could not "commit fornication nor contract matrimony" and was not permitted to "play at cards or dice tables" nor to "haunt taverns or playhouses." Above all, he was not to "waste the goods of his master."]

"I lived at home during the whole of my apprenticeship, and at its completion, had a very fair knowledge of the building business. Immediately after arriving at my twenty-first birthday, I left Mr. Rollings and went to the city *[Peterborough]* where there were more opportunities. In the winter of 1871, I moved again to a still larger city *[Grantham]* where there was an abundance of work for good men."

Voyage to America

"It was in the spring of 1872, while I was working with a number of other men at the bench (most of the work being done by hand at that time), that I first learned of the great Chicago fire in this country. It was reported that large numbers of men were needed to rebuild the city, and this report aroused a good deal of interest among the men in the shop. About half a dozen of us agreed to go to Chicago in the spring of 1872, but when the time to go arrived, all the others backed out. This was a disappointment to me, as I had been in earnest about the matter from the start and had assumed that the others were also. All my plans were made, however, and I decided to go alone.

"About the beginning of April 1872, I set out for the States alone, not knowing a single person on board ship or in the United States. After a tedious voyage lasting about sixteen days, I arrived in New York. Some friends in England had advised me to stop off in Cleveland on my way to Chicago to see some friends of theirs, so I made my way from New York to Cleveland. I was very kindly received there and was persuaded to remain for a time at least, since work was very plentiful. Accordingly, I obtained a job and went to work on a building at the corner of Case and Central Avenues."

[Samuel Austin most likely heard of the Chicago fire early in 1872, for by March of that year he had left his job at Grantham to return to Orton Waterville for a farewell visit. In April he sailed from Liverpool for New York, traveling, like immigrants before and since, in steerage. He paid about £6 for the steamship passage, taking with him his only worldly goods: his carpenter's tools.

Mary Austin, who had heard that the food supplied to steerage passengers was very poor, cooked a ham and some cake to supplement the ship's fare. But, needless to say, her son ate nothing for the first two or three days of his sea voyage. By the time his appetite returned, however, the food that he had taken with him had gone bad, and it had to be thrown overboard. To make matters worse, no bread was served to the emigrants during the entire voyage and they had to put up with hard ship's biscuits and other very plain food.

Samuel Austin arrived in New York harbor before the days of the Statue of Liberty. What he saw, however, was the most pleasing sight he had seen for days—Irish women approaching the ship in boats laden with fresh bread.

The English friends of friends with whom the young carpenter stayed in Cleveland were the Gynn family, and, although his reasons for remaining in Cleveland and abandoning his original destination were undoubtedly economic—Cleveland was one of the fastest growing cities in America—another reason might very well have been the beautiful Miss Sara Jane Gynn, whom he eventually married.]

The Panic of 1873

"In the fall of the following year, 1873, this country went through one of the worst financial panics it has ever suffered and one from which it took six years to recover. Work of every nature was very slack, and I decided to return to the old country for a visit for the winter. Early in the spring of 1874, I returned [*to the States*] and in April went to work for Mr. Vining on Orange St., one of the old builders of the city. I worked continuously for Mr. Vining until the fall of 1877."

[*The panic of 1873 is but one of several economic depressions against which the history of The Austin Company must be told. That conditions had eased sufficiently by early 1874 for Samuel Austin to return to his old job in Cleveland is true enough, although most of the country was still hard in the grip of the general slump. Another reason for his early return was evident: by this time he was already deeply in love with Sarah Jane Gynn.*]

"On June 25, 1874, occurred the greatest event of my life. I was married. In those days, honeymoons were not so popular as they are now; so I was married in the evening, stayed at home the next day and took my wife rowing on the Cuyahoga River, and the following day went back to work.

"Meanwhile, in a business way, matters were gradually becoming worse. Carpenters were working for $1.50 per day and working three or four days a week in the summer, and scarcely at all in the winter. These were real hard times. Finally in 1877, having heard that there was plenty of work in England, I decided to return there for a time until conditions in this country should improve.

"We had two children at that time, our oldest daughter, now Mrs. Dr. Manchester, and Wilbert J. Austin (now Vice-President and General Manager of The Austin Company). We stayed in England for about two years, and during most of the time I was in a small business for myself, developing and making a pleating machine [*first suggested by Mrs. Austin*] which affected a great saving of labor in large dressmaking establishments. I had a small shop and made the machines myself, finding a very ready sale for them in the nearby cities and towns. This was my first experience in sales work, and although it was in a small way, I obtained some very valuable experience.

"As the demand for these machines grew, it became necessary

for me to make much longer trips over England and Wales. These trips sometimes lasted for several days or a week and were fraught with all manner of difficulties and obstacles. By dint of much effort, however, the business eventually was successful, both financially and as a valuable experience."

[The year 1878, consequently, is a watershed year in the life of Samuel Austin, marking his establishment as an entrepreneur. It is typical of the man that the panic of 1873 should have led directly to his profiting from adversity.]

"Upon my return from a trip to Ireland, I learned that things in a business way were improving in the States, so we decided to return. Prior to my departure for England in 1877, we had purchased a home in Cleveland, which we rented while we were away. Our furniture had been stored, so we had a home to return to. Mrs. Austin's family all lived in Cleveland, so that we were very glad to come back again. My own father and mother and only sister remained in England, and when I left them to return to Cleveland, it was the last time I ever saw my dear father. Though people of moderate means, my parents were of the highest type morally and spiritually. All that I am, I owe to their noble leadership in life, example, and training."

The Early Years

"Upon my return to Cleveland in 1879, I went to work at once for my old boss, Mr. J. Vining, and continued to work for him until 1881. In the fall of that year, I was asked by Mr. A. J. Cook, a doctor and friend of ours, to take a contract for a small addition and alteration to his house on Broadway near Forest St., now 37th St. From that time until the present, there has never been a time when The Austin Company did not have one or more contracts on hand. The first job was very satisfactory all around. Dr. Cook was pleased and recommended me to others. In this way, I became acquainted with Dr. Cook's druggist, a Mr. Hechler, who proved a good friend and helper. Another man who was of considerable help to me in the early days was Mr. O. M. Stafford, now President of the Cleveland Worsted Mills and 1st V. P. of the Broadway and Woodland Avenue Bank. At that time, he was in the real estate and insurance business. Our business interests were mutual. I plugged hard for him, especially for insurance, and he helped me to obtain contracts for building. He was also connected with the

Commercial National Bank and suggested that I do my banking with his firm. I followed this suggestion.

"At that time, our methods of operation were very simple. Almost all of the work was done on the lump sum basis, which did not require much bookkeeping. Cost keeping was poorly taken care of, in fact, one did not have time to look after these things. Most of the work at that time was house work. I would take a contract for a house, place a foreman on the job, haul all the light material myself, by means of a horse and light wagon, and have the dealers do the balance. All estimating was done in the evening. Later, Mr. W. B. Stewart, now our attorney, then a boy going to school, helped me evenings and Saturdays. Many a night I have been up until midnight and after, and out again with the men next morning at starting time, seeing that they had all the necessary material on the work and not giving them any excuse for loafing on the job. Competition was very keen, and one had to use every reasonable effort to push the job along."

[The common sight of Samuel Austin driving his horse and wagon through the streets of Cleveland in the 1880s is confirmed in the memoirs of an early employee who adds: "Many times we used the horse to hoist materials to the roof and upper stories of the jobs in those days." The young schoolboy, W. B. Stewart, became years later one of the company's first stockholders when it was incorporated in 1904; his sister Ida married Wilbert J. Austin.]

"In regard to methods of development, I found that a satisfied customer is the best advertisement and security for future work. That meant good material and best workmanship. At first, most of my work was done in the neighborhood in which I lived, and this constant association with the people for whom I worked was in itself an incentive to honest and fair dealing. I soon began to receive preference in my work, and as I came to figure in architects' offices, many owners would insist on my being given preference over others."

The First Shop — "About two years after commencing business, I found it necessary to purchase land for a shop, and I decided upon the corner of Broadway and Gallup Sts. for its location. The lot had a front on Broadway of 56 feet and extended back on Gallup St. for 175 feet. Shortly afterwards I purchased 56 feet adjoining, making the lot 112′ x 175′. In the rear of this corner lot, I built our first shop, of which I have a picture in my office today. It was surprising the amount of work which was turned out in this small building. At first all work was done by hand, though later I purchased a hand power rip saw, which is now in use in our present mill. This was quite a labor saver. As the volume of business increased, it became necessary to enlarge the shop and electric power was employed, and one of the best motors we have at the present mill today is the ten horsepower motor which I purchased about 25 years ago. From that time, until we moved into our 152nd St. mill, the shop was always too small, although enlarged again and again. Small orders were profitable."

[*By stating that he "found it necessary" to build a shop, Samuel Austin is being typically modest. The fact is that with his business beginning to prosper, he was now buying enough millwork to be plagued with problems of price and quality. He decided, therefore, to set up his own shop to supply sash, doors, and other millwork for the houses on which he held the general contract. This small shop stood directly behind the Austin residence, which, when Cleveland eventually numbered its streets, was given the address of 4401 Broadway.*

The East 152nd Street mill was built in 1912. The saw and motor mentioned in the narrative are included in the inventory of Samuel Austin's goods that accompanied the original papers of incorporation in 1904 drawn up by W. B. Stewart, and the photograph of his first shop that Samuel Austin displayed so proudly in his office years later is here reproduced.]

"The men seen in the photo are some of the earliest employees of the company. Henry Cline, the man at the corner of the building, is the oldest man. He was a good faithful man but lacked the staying qualities of some of the others whom I had. He still works as a carpenter. The man in the center is our old and faithful employee, Henry Dippel. No one knows better than myself the important part he played in making our company what it is today, and our company recognizes a lasting obligation to him. Other good men, such as Samuel Kirkham, Ernest Finke, and Rudolph Wertheim, were with us for many years and we shall never forget them."

[*Samuel Austin's respect for his employees and his acknowledgement of their importance to the growth and well-being of his*

Samuel Austin's first carpentry shop, c. 1883.

company, an attitude hardly typical of his time, developed eventually into a unique plan of employee ownership of the company that will be discussed in a subsequent chapter.]

A Temperance Man

"No one who has not gone through the experience knows the amount of work it is possible for a man to perform under stress and pressure. Being young, full of ambition, anxious to make good, and having a determination to do the very best work in the neighborhood, I was able, through the faithful help of those working with me, to achieve success in a measure far beyond my expectations. Some of the principles which guided me were honest work, good buildings, strict Sunday observance, strict temperance. Liquor was suppressed and I gave preference to temperate men.

"To illustrate: I was invited to bid by the owner on a brick block at the corner of Broadway and 34th Street, C. E. Richardson, architect. The bids were to be given to the owner, who kept a grocery store with a saloon in the rear. I delivered my bid in person on Saturday evening. The other bidders spent Sunday in the saloon trying to get the job. The owner finally told them that if he wanted to sell whiskey, he needed drinking men to buy it, but when he wanted a building, he wanted a temperance man to put it up. On Monday he gave me the job."

[Samuel Austin's almost legendary teetotalism was not without its humorous side, as he himself would have been the first to admit. The following is from a 1921 interview in a business magazine: "In the early days of house building, a very curious custom prevailed. As soon as the frame was up, the men would fasten the branch of a tree to the ridge-pole, which was the signal for a 'treat' by the boss. A treat in those days meant beer. The first time a tree branch was raised over one of Austin's houses, he called his men together and said: 'I recognize the signal, but you know I am opposed to any kind of liquor; however, I will give you a treat.' Half an hour later he appeared with a basket of oranges which he passed around." Lest anyone miss the generosity of Samuel Austin's temperance "treat," an orange would have been considerably more rare in the Cleveland of the 1880s than a pail of beer.]

"With reference to Sunday observance, while the business was under my own personal care, I never did any work of any kind

Mr. and Mrs. Samuel Austin and their five children at 4401 Broadway, c. 1884.

on Sunday, except for looking after my fires and the fires in the heating plants for the mill. Many times the matter was put up to me, but I always found a way out by working late Saturday night and going early Monday morning. I was often requested to figure on Sunday and I positively refused. I firmly believe that in such cases, the men who asked me to figure had more respect for me refusing, because I often got the work.

"Like most growing concerns, we were often short of cash and had to hustle collections. And yet I remember a good customer of mine bringing me a considerable payment on Sunday to the house, and as much as I needed the cash, I asked him to take it back, saying that I would come after it any place he might designate during the week. This he did and he was always a friend of mine afterwards. This may seem a somewhat old-fashioned way of doing business, but these are the principles on which The Austin Company is built."

Early Buildings

"Some of the early buildings which I built were the Schaffer Training School on Fowler St. near Broadway, frame and brick stores, and buildings on Broadway from one end to the other. The Erdman store was one of the first, on Broadway near 37th Street. The Troyan block, one of the largest on Broadway, just beyond 37th Street, the Broadway Bank, cor. Broadway and 55th St., and the South Cleveland Bank. Several of these buildings were designed by Henry Dippel.

"Among the early factory buildings which we built are the factory buildings for the Canfield Oil Company, the Buckeye Electric Company (before they consolidated with the General Electric Company), the Western Mineral Wool Company block in Cleveland and Chicago, this being my first out of town work, and the Cleveland Worsted Mills Co. Most of these buildings we designed ourselves."

[Although photographs of several of these early Austin buildings are lost in history, others have been preserved and are included in the gallery following this chapter. That "most of these buildings" were Austin-designed is significant evidence that the Austin Method was already germinating in the late nineteenth century.

The construction of the Broadway Savings Bank in 1889 was of particular importance. Industrial executives among the bank's

A rare photograph (c. 1902) of the Broadway Bank Building.

clientele now had a first-hand acquaintance with Austin's high quality workmanship and were drawn to him to construct their own commercial and industrial buildings. One of these clients led directly to Austin's "first out of town work" in 1895—in Chicago, the city that had originally drawn him to America twenty-three years earlier.

The reference to a building for an electric company in the catalogue of early Austin factory buildings is tantalizing in its reticence, for The Austin Company was soon to rise to prominence through its work in this burgeoning field. In the fall of 1895, shortly after his son had enrolled as a student of mechanical engineering at what is now Case Institute of Technology, Samuel Austin received the contract for Cleveland's first electric lamp factory.]

The Samuel Austin & Son Company

"About this time, my son, Wilbert J. Austin, having graduated from Case School and having served a year in post-graduate work in Cleveland and abroad, decided to cast in his lot with me. We organized ourselves into a stock company, known as the Samuel Austin & Son Co. The combination of young red blood and technical knowledge with my own past experience enabled us to do real team work, and with the noble efforts of our numerous and faithful employees, brought the business to its present state."

[In 1899 Wilbert J. Austin graduated from the Case School of Applied Science with a bachelor of science degree in mechanical engineering. After teaching higher mathematics for a semester at Case and serving briefly as Cleveland's assistant smoke inspector, he spent a year studying architecture in England and on the Continent, returning in 1901 to Cleveland, where he joined his father's business. After three years together, this partnership of father and son was formalized by incorporation on May 7, 1904 as The Samuel Austin & Son Company, with a capitalization of $25,000.]

The Austin Method Evolves

Thus Samuel Austin's otherwise complete narrative breaks off without a *direct* word about the origin of the company's most famous innovation, the Austin Method. Recent tradition has it that the idea of the "undivided responsibility" contract, with one organization handling all activities of design, engineering, and construction, originated in 1911. Actually, the conception is considerably older. Its historic antecedent, in fact, is one of the *oldest* architectural traditions—that of the carpenter-builder.

The Samuel Austin & Son Company's first publication on the subject—a handsome hardbound book entitled *The Austin Method*, and released in 1913—states that "The Austin Method has been in operation since 1901." Although this early date is difficult to prove—or to disprove—several reasons suggest why it may very well be accurate. For one thing, the seed for the idea had already been planted in the '90s, when Samuel Austin's contracting company had both designed and constructed several of its buildings. For another, the Austin trademark—two wonderfully stylized initials combined to represent the *A* and *M* in "Austin Method"—is also believed to have come into being in 1911. This, too, is actually of older vintage, having first been used on company letterheads in early 1909 and most probably having been designed in 1908. And, since no fiscally conservative organization would possibly employ an untried, untested, or unsuccessful innovation as its logotype, one must conclude that the Austin Method had already been long-established by 1908. Finally, it is almost certain that Wilbert Austin—a bright young man, gifted with a talent for organization and an eagerness to employ his engineering know-how to advange—had been directly responsible for formalizing the notion of a system that combined architectural and engineering service with construction. That this may have been his plan as early as 1901—the very year he joined his father's firm—is entirely possible.

A recent search of the Austin archives reveals that the Austin Method was advertised in Cleveland newspapers as early as 1907. "The Austin Method," one announcement read, "is a square deal way of planning, erecting, equipping and maintaining buildings. It makes you in effect your own architect, engineer and builder, plus our specialized knowledge, experience and facilities." What the business community's response to this ungrammatical, but nonetheless succinct, advertisement might have been is difficult to ascertain. Contemporary corporate records provide no clue since the minutes for the period are blank. And no wonder. The panic of 1907, even worse than that of 1873, was in full swing, causing business to slow to a trickle and postponing in all likelihood the rapid progress of the nascent Austin Method.

Austin and the Incandescent Lamp

The panic of 1907 severely affected the development of most American business. Relatively untouched, however, was one industry which Samuel Austin must have thanked a benevolent Providence for having strategically situated in Cleveland: the manufacturing of electric light bulbs.

The history of the early incandescent lamp—which is closely linked with that of The Austin Company—centers on improvements in its filament. In the first practical lamps, carbon filaments had been used, and carbon had no real rival until the appearance first of the osmium lamp in 1898, then of the tantalum lamp in 1903, and finally of tungsten in 1904 as the most suitable filament material. These rapid developments led directly to improvements in the manufacture of the whole lamp. The earlier lamps had all been handmade. By the end of the first decade of the twentieth century, however, there arose a pressing need for automatic production as electrification spread rapidly through the cities of America.

In 1908, consequently, The Samuel Austin & Son Company began to construct a series of electric lamp factories for various manufacturers. Then, in 1910, it undertook a large number of projects for the National Electric Lamp Association, not long before it was absorbed by the General Electric Company. In rapid succession, contracts were let for Austin-designed, Austin-engineered, and Austin-built plants in Cleveland, Warren, Youngstown, Niles, and Shelby, Ohio; Providence and Central Falls, Rhode Island; St. Louis, Missouri; Minneapolis, Minnesota; and Oakland, California, among other cities. Within the space of two years, then, the idea of "undivided responsibility" was beginning to take hold—and in many isolated spots across the nation. With its volume of construction now steadily increasing, Austin was obliged in 1911 to move its offices to rented quarters in the Wise Building, at the corner of Euclid Avenue and East 65th Street.

Nela Park and the Nelite Plant

With a wealth of experience in planning new electric light facilities behind it, Austin was offered a dramatic opportunity late in 1911, when B. G. Tremaine of the National Electric Lamp Association awarded it contracts for the erection of their extensive research facilities at Nela Park and for the design and construction of a capacious new lamp manufacturing plant. These projects were the largest the Austins had ever undertaken. Each was within a mile of the other on Cleveland's east side. And both were to make The Austin Company a name to conjure with.

Their rented offices now completely outgrown after only eighteen months of occupancy, the Austins moved their base of operation to Euclid Avenue and Noble Road in the spring of 1913. There, within the view of both new projects, they built what was to serve as the company's general headquarters for the next forty-seven years. And there, that same year, they celebrated the success of the Austin Method by publishing an illustrated sixty-page book about their innovation:

> The Austin Method placed building on a square-deal basis. With mutual confidence, the interests of owner and builder became identical. The owner guaranteed the builder fair pay for his services; and the builder guaranteed the owner a fair return on his money.
>
> The Austin Method has been in operation since 1901. It has controlled the erection of buildings from Rhode Island to California.
>
> It has held old customers—three-fourths of last year's work on repeat-orders.
>
> It has made new customers, creating a business that now requires the services of more than a thousand men.
>
> And it has created a complete organization capable of handling big operations—twelve buildings for one customer erected last year under the Austin Method, and twelve more for the same customer now under way.

Samuel Austin had come a long way from Orton Waterville.

The high quality of Samuel Austin's work attracted many industrialists who patronized several bank offices he built in Cleveland in the late nineteenth century. Note the ornate Art Nouveau wood paneling and brass tellers' cages in the offices of the South Cleveland Banking Company (c. 1900) *below. Opposite:* Construction of the Niles Glass Works, Niles, Ohio, c. 1910.

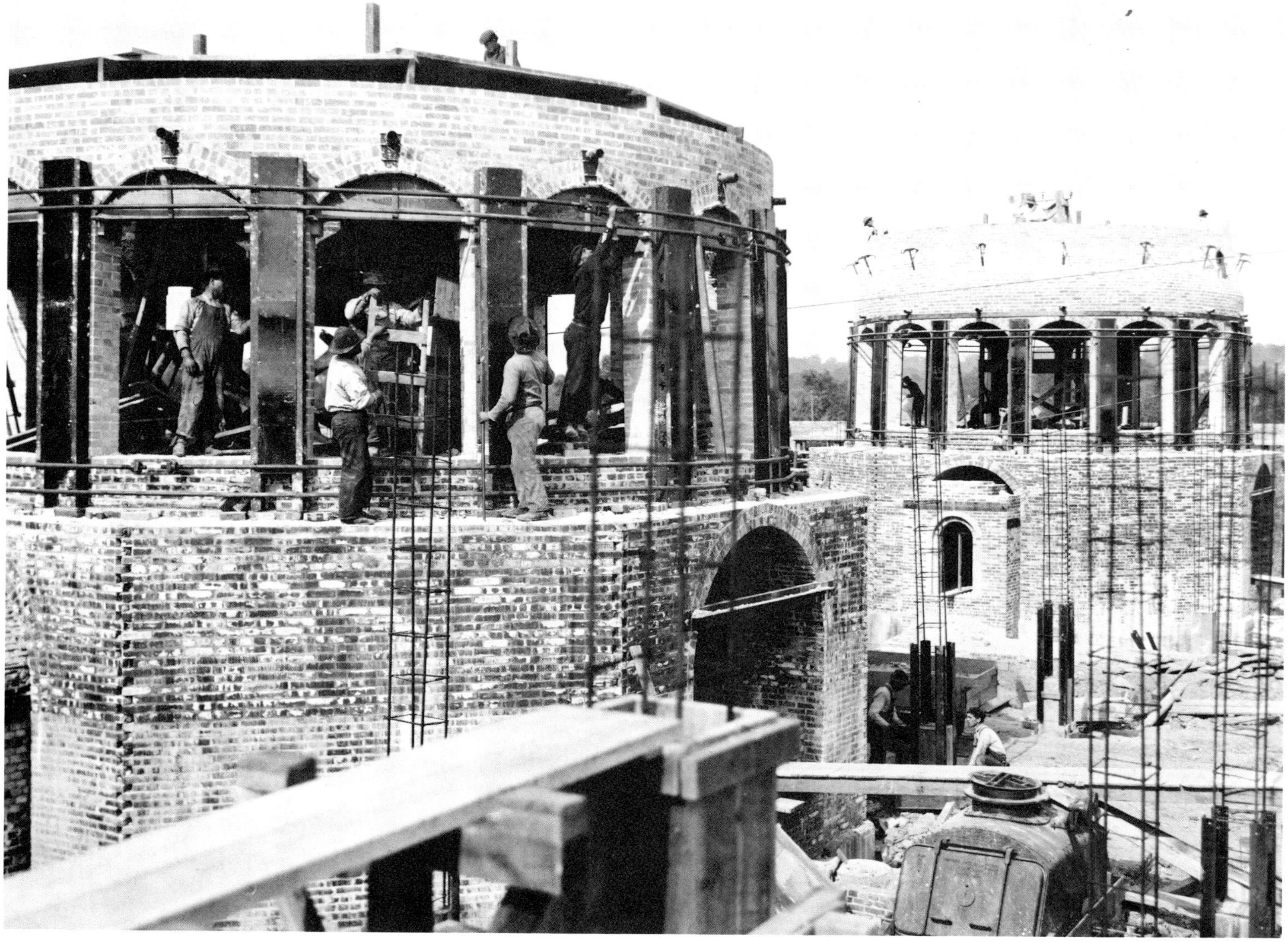

In his autobiographical memoir Samuel Austin mentions the many "frame and brick stores and buildings [he erected] on Broadway from one end to the other." Coulton's (c. 1900) was one of them.

Other early Austin buildings included the Wooltex cloak factory for the H. Black Co. (c. 1906)—the first reinforced concrete structure in Cleveland, *above*; the Adams Bag Company factory, Chagrin Falls, Ohio (1912), *left*; an early sawtooth structure for the Cleveland Metal Products Co. (1912), *opposite (above)*; and a multi-story building for the same company (1912), *opposite (below)*.

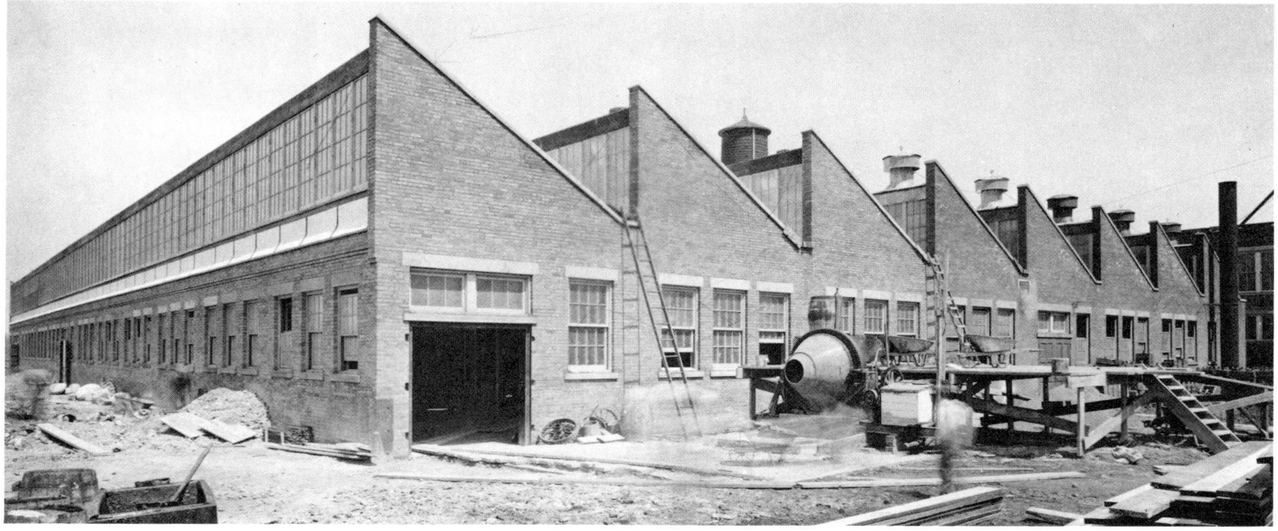

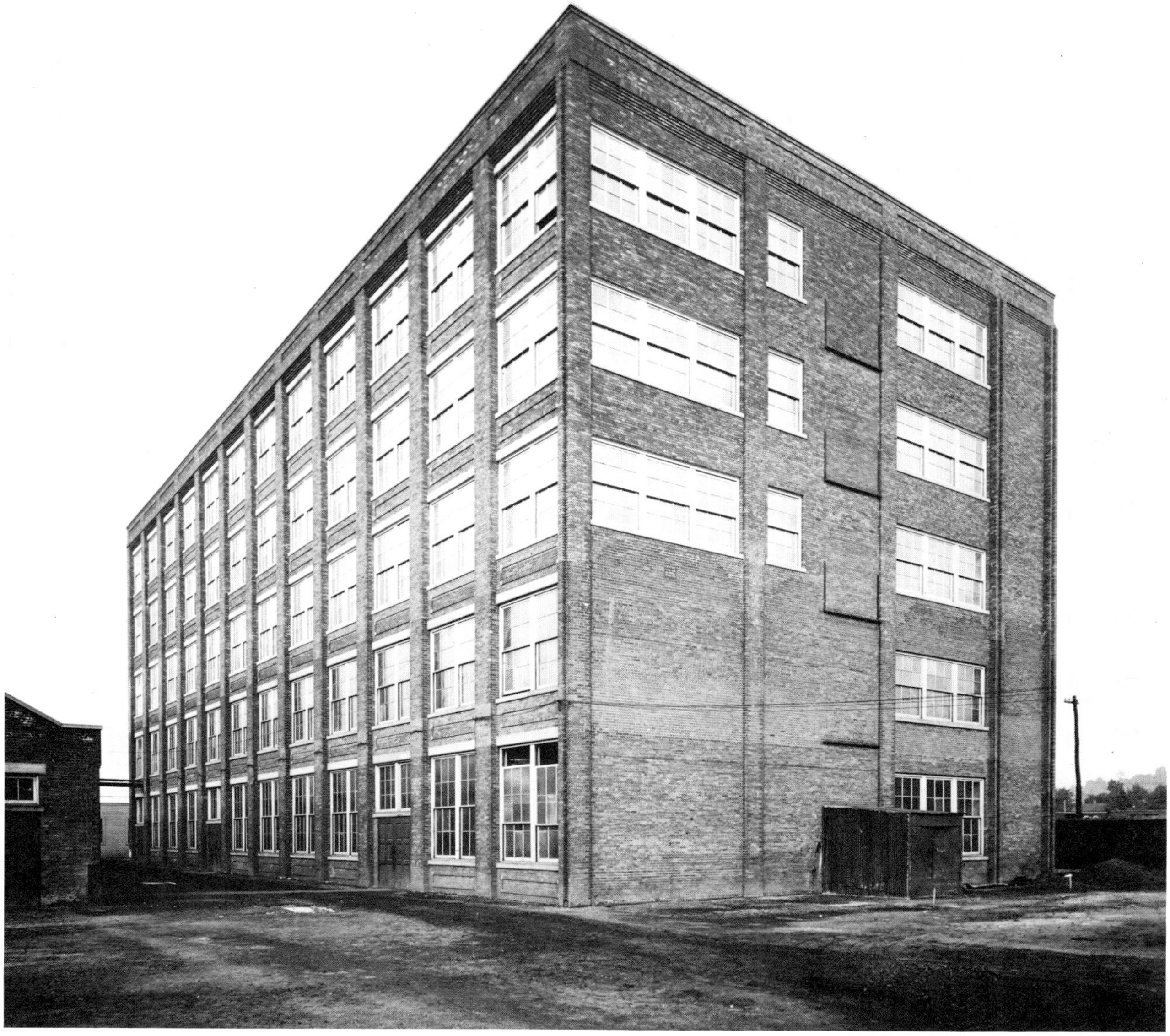

Samuel Austin established his reputation for fine workmanship by building some of the most beautiful homes in Cleveland and its surrounding suburbs. The suburban mansion, *above*, dates from the same period (c. 1911) as the apartment building, *right*, one of many erected and owned by The Samuel Austin & Son Company. At this time the company was beginning to make a name for itself as builders for the incandescent lamp industry. *Opposite:* Construction of a factory for the Youngstown (Ohio) Mazda Lamp Co., 1912.

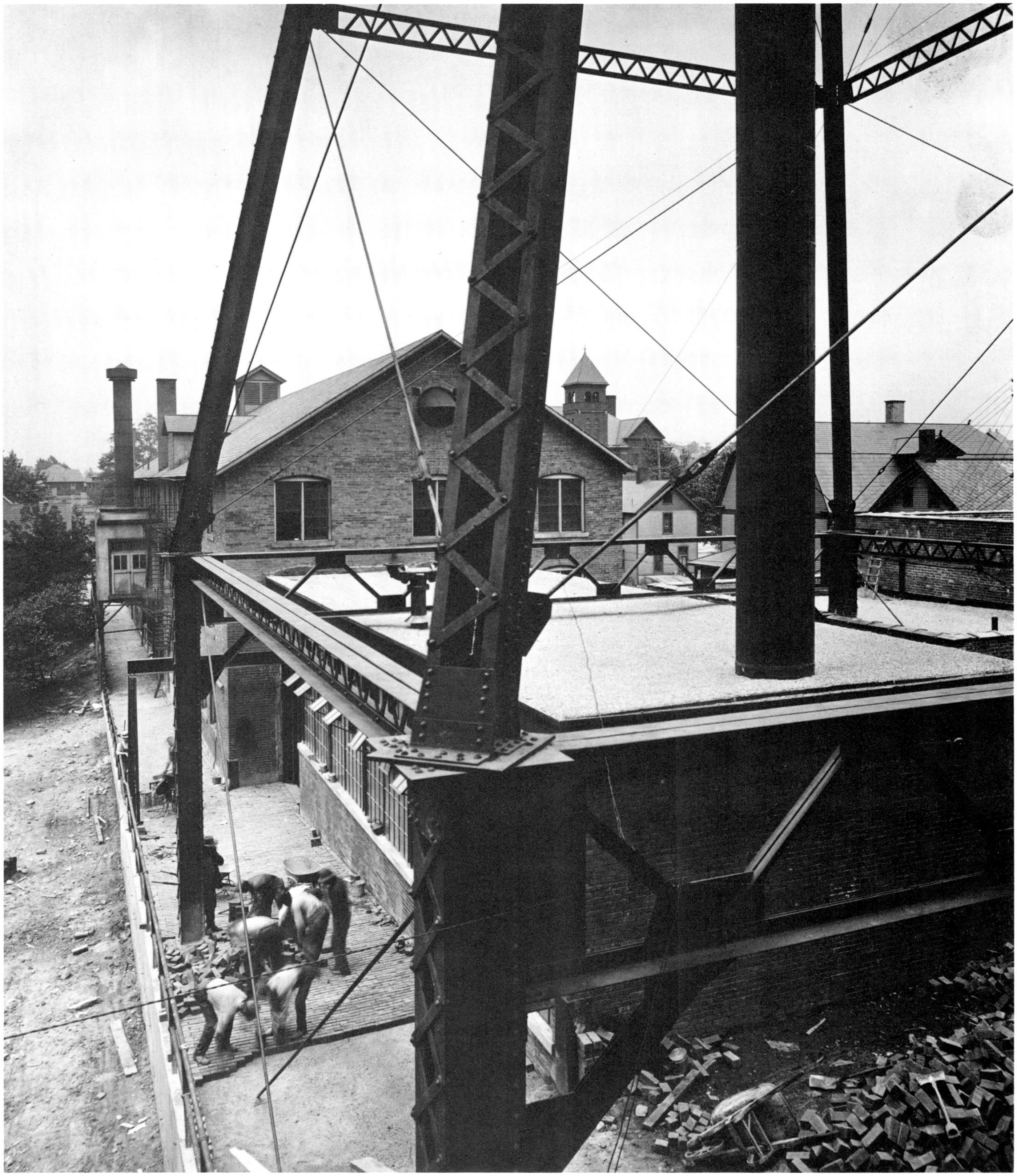

Work for the National Electric Lamp Association not only proved the effectiveness of the Austin Method, but led directly to the development of standardization in industrial building by 1914. *Above:* Incandescent lamp plant, National Lamp Works, Oakland, California (1910). *Opposite (above):* Building the Central Falls (Rhode Island) Lamp Works (1913). *Opposite (below):* Employees cafeteria, Ohio Lamp Works, Warren, Ohio (1911).

45

Nela Park, Cleveland, Ohio. This Austin-engineered research laboratory for the General Electric Company, erected in 1913, introduced the "campus" idea which is followed today in the layout of many outstanding industrial research centers. Wallace & Goodwillie were the consulting architects.

47

An increasing volume of work for the National Electric Lamp Association enabled The Samuel Austin & Son Company to design and build its new offices, *below,* on Euclid Avenue and Noble Road in 1913 and to build a new mill on East 152nd Street, *opposite,* in 1912.

49

50

As early as 1913 Austin advertised that it had "its own equipment for heavy construction work—locomotive cranes, traction cranes, heavy-duty mixers, and all kinds of miscellaneous light equipment." *From left:* Peerless auto truck with trailer, unloading brick (1913); O-2 shovel (1912); locomotive crane (1912); Packard truck (c. 1913); Peerless auto truck with trailer (1913).

By World War I, Austin had contributed distinctively modern architectural forms to America's dramatically changing industrial landscape. *Above:* German-American Portland Cement Works, La Salle, Illinois (1916). *Below:* The Gair Company plant dominates the nineteenth-century town of Piermont, New York (1919).

An Austin Company picnic at the Willoughby, Ohio, home of Samuel Austin, c. 1916.

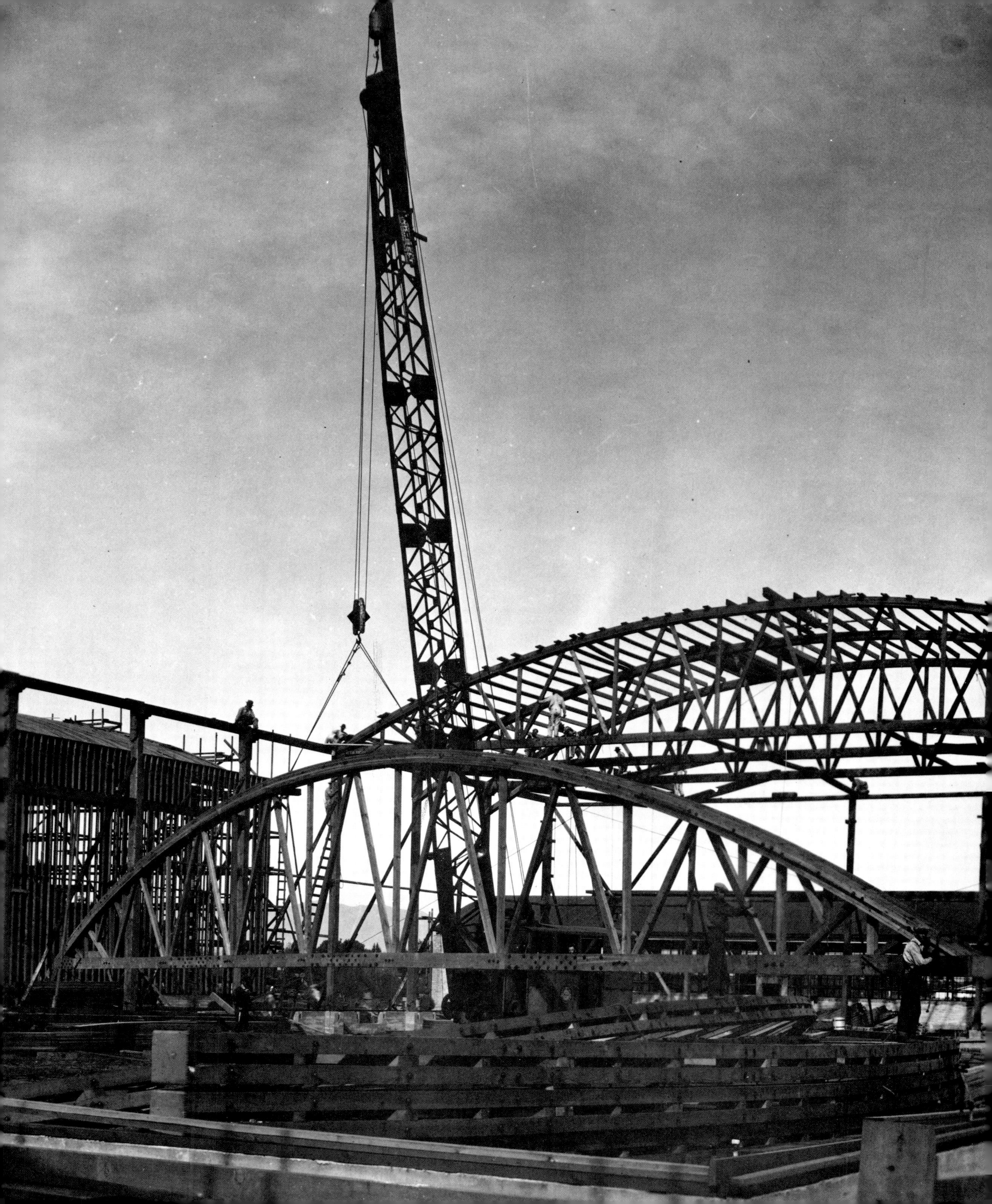

II Speed and Standardization

The Development of Standardization

For the contemporary reader, the remote and innocent years in which the Austin Method evolved are difficult to contemplate, much less to understand. Most of us, after all, now take technological civilization for granted.

Early Technology

But to Americans living through the first decade of the twentieth century—a period culturally and politically very much like the nineteenth—modern technology was virtually the only thing "new"—and it was tremendously exciting. It was the time of the great international exhibitions, in every one of which a new "miracle" of technical invention had created a sensation. And it was the time, too, of almost unbounded faith in the benevolence of technological progress. One by one, the great inventions of the late nineteenth century were emerging in improved and practical form: the electric light, the telephone, the moving picture, the phonograph, the automobile. And, in its first ten years, the young century had already witnessed the development of things even more inexplicable: wireless telegraphy, the vacuum tube, the airplane. All the excitement, however, merely focused on the novelty of *things*. That these things could and would have an impact on society and on the way people behaved and thought had not yet occurred to many. Not too many years beyond these halcyon days, however, lay a war in which the gallantry of men and stupidity of officers were to be indiscriminately mocked by the new technology of warfare. These, too, were *things*.

Opposite: Erecting the 110-foot timber trusses for one of Hollywood's first sound stages, Mack Sennett's Studio City, 1927.

But at the beginning of the twentieth century—just as The Samuel Austin & Son Company was starting to come into its own —modern technology, as exciting as it was to the initiated, still played only a minor role in the lives of most Americans, the majority of whom were then still farmers or artisans living either in the countryside or in small towns. The tools they used and the life they led were pre-industrial, and they remained unaware of the modern technology that was growing up so rapidly about them. Only in a few large cities had modern technology and its new inventions imposed themselves upon daily life. And Cleveland was one of them.

Cleveland in 1910

By 1910 Cleveland was the sixth largest city in the United States and a rapidly growing industrial capital—the home of John D.

Rockefeller's Standard Oil Company and a center for the production of iron and steel, chemicals, paints and varnishes, machine tools, boats, wagons, bicycles, sewing machines, ready-to-wear clothing, and electrical parts. It had only recently lost its standing as the world's leading manufacturer of motor cars, although it continued to produce some eighty different makes of automobiles for the next two decades. And it led the world in the production of the incandescent lamp—an unchallenged prominence clearly reflected in an Austin inventory of 1913:

> *List of buildings completed for The National Lamp Co.*
>
> The Buckeye Plant, at E. 45th Street, Cleveland.
> *Five buildings, including a power house, office and three factory buildings.*
>
> Nela Park.
> *Eight buildings, including Engineering, Sales, Administration, Purchasing and Garage combined; Power House, Dr. Hyde's Laboratory, Working Laboratory and camp buildings.*
>
> Nelite Factory, E. 152nd Street, Cleveland.
> *Eight buildings, including Power House, five factory buildings and two warehouses.*
>
> Minneapolis, 2 *buildings*
> Oakland, Cal., 2 *buildings*
> Central Falls, R. I., 2 *buildings*
> Ohio Warren Plant, 4 *buildings*
> Trumbull Warren Plant, 3 *buildings*
> Ravenna, 1 *building*
> Shelby, 2 *buildings*
> St. Louis, 4 *buildings*
> Youngstown, 3 *buildings*
> Niles, 3 *buildings*
> Fostoria, 1 *building*
> R. I. Glass, 3 *buildings*
> Conneaut, 2 *buildings*
>
> Making a total of 53 buildings, which cost approximately $5,000,000.

The real value of five million dollars to a young company that had been incorporated only nine years before should be reckoned in contemporary terms. In 1913 an unskilled laborer in the employ of The Samuel Austin & Son Company would have worked ten hours daily, six days a week—from 7:00 A.M. to 5:30 P.M., including an unpaid thirty-minute break for lunch—for a wage of twenty cents an hour, or a weekly salary of twelve dollars. A journeyman carpenter would have earned roughly twice that hourly rate, but would have worked an eight-hour day for a slightly less than twenty-dollar weekly wage. But with those hard-earned 1913 dollars, the same workmen would be able to purchase a brand-new union suit for only twenty-two cents, a linen collar for seven cents, or even a complete three-piece bedroom suite for the princely sum of $14.95. By any reckoning, then, five million dollars was in those days a great deal of money. And it brought into being, for a growing public eager to be served, an uncountable number of early incandescent lamps.

A Crisis Is Solved

If The Samuel Austin & Son Company had made its name through work for the burgeoning electric lamp industry, then it soon faced its first major crisis because of it, as well. A rapidly changing technology had in an astonishingly short period of time forced a need for more and more electric lamp factories. Now, just as suddenly, that same surge of technology had produced an improved light bulb so reliable and commercially sound that by the close of 1913 the urgent need for new plant expansion had ended. The new year looked bleak indeed: Austin faced 1914 with a crying need for work.

Ironically, the solution to this vexing problem lay inherent in the problem itself. The sheer volume of work that Austin had undertaken for the electric lamp industry had required a degree of standardization to enable the projects to be completed with speed and efficiency. If standardization had solved some of yesterday's problems, it was now about to be impressed to solve today's. Wilbert J. Austin—who, by this time, had already come to be called W. J. by the people in his employ—is credited with having originated the idea of the standard steel-frame factory building, an idea that revolutionized American industrial construction and added new depth and meaning to the Austin Method.

The First Standard Factory Buildings

The basic idea behind standardization developed from W. J. Austin's shrewd observation of changes almost everywhere about him, in particular of an economic change ubiquitous in American society as it emerged from the chrysalis of the nineteenth century: the variety of American production, the sheer volume of individual design, was apparently diminishing in number. A manufacturer of saws, for example, would reduce his line of 250 models as soon as he understood that fewer than 25 would meet the average laborer's needs. Similarly, a plowmaker's line of 200 models would be reduced when he understood that a mere 15 would answer the average farmer's needs. Therefore, W. J. Austin reasoned that a very large portion of the country's factory-building needs could be fully met with a comparatively few standard-building units. The consequence of this logical deduction is far-reaching: Standardization lowers costs, advances capital returns, conserves labor, and increases production. In short, it makes good economic sense. It is hardly surprising, then, that the Austin program of standard industrial buildings came into being when it did. It was clearly an idea whose time had come. The wonder is that it took so long. After all, having reached a similar conclusion, Henry Ford had come up with the Model T six years before.

The analogy is really not at all far-fetched. The Austin standard industrial building *was* the Model T of the construction world. Both were inexpensive. Both were built in record time. Both were exceptionally long-lived conceptions. And both made their creators very rich men. But there was withal one substantial difference: there was only one Model T—and that one came in black—while there were ten Austin standard buildings—and these could even be custom-made. This combination of interchangeable standard units to affect a variety of designs anticipated modular construction by many years.

Speed In one respect, at least, the advent of the Austin standard building reinforced an essential tenet of the Austin Method: *economy through speed*. In its 1913 publication on the Method, Austin had warned potential clients of the folly of old-fashioned building contracts: "While you're waiting for plans, specifications, and contractors' estimates, you lose more than any saving on the building could possibly amount to. Under the Austin Method, you can proceed at once, without loss of time, and yet be absolutely sure of getting your building at reasonable cost." If in 1913 the company promised that "plans could be drawn and accepted while the excavation was being made," the adoption of standardization the following year enabled it to promise the structural steel for delivery the day after signing the contract. This unprecedented speed was made possible by the fabrication of steel for standard designs on a production basis long in advance of contracts. Such steel, ready for immediate use, was stocked by Austin in various parts of the country. At first the steel was fabricated *for* Austin. Very soon, as the idea of standard industrial designs caught on, steel was fabricated *by* Austin at its own fabricating shop, Bliss Mill. And as the builder's costs came down, so did those of the owner.

1916: A Key Year

From the start, then, the standard building program met with a warm reception. In early 1915, for example, its praises were sung by the president of the Philadelphia Chamber of Commerce who hailed its benefits: "manufacture on a quantity basis, equalization of production over slack periods, reduction of maintenance costs, elimination of poor design, reduction of labor and machine costs, closer cooperation, and a uniform degree of safety and efficiency during and after construction." But no one really anticipated the almost phenomenal popularity it reached the following year when four events occurred that, taken all together, conspired to end abruptly the nascent period of Austin's history:

1. No fewer than eleven construction companies followed the lead of Austin engineers in inaugurating standard designs of their own, providing evidence of the extent to which the idea of standardization had influenced American industrial thought in general.

2. In order to handle an increasing volume of demand for its standard buildings, Austin became the first engineering and construction company to establish sales offices in strategic industrial centers—namely, Detroit and Jackson, Michigan; Philadelphia and Pittsburgh, Pennsylvania; and Bridgeport, Connecticut—an innovation that led eventually to the development of a network of district offices from coast to coast.

3. Austin began to advertise nationally, not only in the recognized building and technical trade journals, but in full-page and double-page spreads appearing in the most popular magazines of the day—*The Literary Digest* and *The Saturday Evening Post*. In so doing, it became the first industrial engineering and building firm to seek an audience within the pages of the popular press.

4. Given the flattery of its competitors' conscious imitation, the practical reality of several offices beyond the boundaries of Cleveland, and the national prestige of advertisements in major magazines, the name Austin now implied far more than the con-

tributions of Samuel and Wilbert J. alone. Consequently, on April 11, 1916, The Samuel Austin & Son Company became officially The Austin Company.

A year later, almost to the day, America was off to war.

World War I All the elements that have been considered thus far in the history of The Austin Company seemed, almost as if by some preternatural force, to converge at the crossroads of the First World War, a tragic but inexorable event that buried the final vestiges of the nineteenth century and established once and for all the awesome might of the new technology of the twentieth. Almost as if the developments of the previous forty years had served as a dress rehearsal for an actual performance upon the stage of history, Austin—with the rest of the nation—responded to an urgent call to arms.

In the face of a large demand for industrial buildings to produce the implements of war, Austin was in the forefront from the start. Its reputation for economy, reliability, and speed, and its Method that assured professional competence in every stage of construction, from engineering to building to equipment—in short, from planning to production—made it a vital element in America's technological mobilization of the home front.

Within the twenty months of war, during which government restrictions prohibited all nonessential building and eventually banned the use of steel, requiring in turn the rapid conversion of the standard building program from steel to wood, Austin's number of offices grew to eight, its steel fabrication mill was enlarged, its volume of business increased by almost thirty-five percent, it undertook a series of projects for the nation's railroads that continued long after the war, and constructed several major military installations for the federal government—gaining experience that would hold it in good stead two decades later at the outbreak of another war.

Military Projects One of these military facilities was the massive Frankford Arsenal in Philadelphia. Shortly before the war, in 1916, when the arsenal was already under construction, Army engineers had blatantly copied the plans of an Austin Standard No. 5 building and had sent it out to bids, awarding the contract finally to the lowest bidder—

The Austin Company. The nearest competitor had wanted 105 days in which to complete the 60-day job.

Other notable government projects included, among others, the Naval Aircraft Factory at the Philadelphia Navy Yard and four Navy radio towers at Annapolis, Maryland. These 600-foot steel transmitting stations were then the most high-powered in the world and controlled the entire Atlantic fleet throughout the war. In the spring of 1917, Austin supervised the mass shipment of thirteen Standard No. 3 buildings from the newly-expanded Bliss Mill to Newport News, Virginia, and thence to France where the units were to be erected for use as Army motor transport repair shops. The entire shipment contained 170 railroad freight cars of material and surely merits notation in the history of prefabrication still to be written.

The Curtiss Aircraft Plant

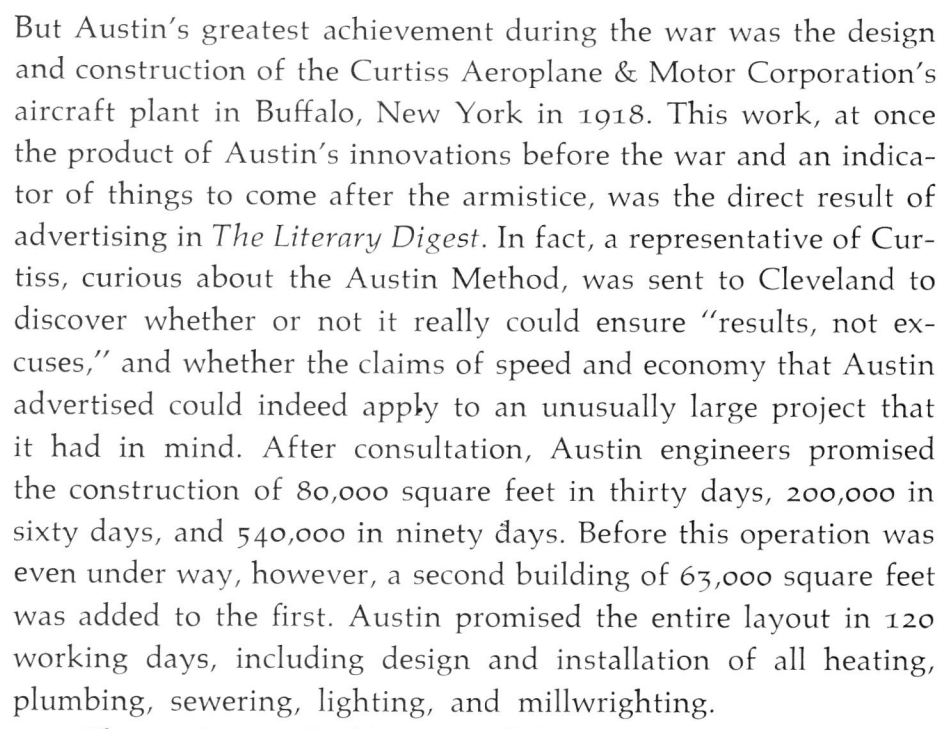

But Austin's greatest achievement during the war was the design and construction of the Curtiss Aeroplane & Motor Corporation's aircraft plant in Buffalo, New York in 1918. This work, at once the product of Austin's innovations before the war and an indicator of things to come after the armistice, was the direct result of advertising in *The Literary Digest*. In fact, a representative of Curtiss, curious about the Austin Method, was sent to Cleveland to discover whether or not it really could ensure "results, not excuses," and whether the claims of speed and economy that Austin advertised could indeed apply to an unusually large project that it had in mind. After consultation, Austin engineers promised the construction of 80,000 square feet in thirty days, 200,000 in sixty days, and 540,000 in ninety days. Before this operation was even under way, however, a second building of 63,000 square feet was added to the first. Austin promised the entire layout in 120 working days, including design and installation of all heating, plumbing, sewering, lighting, and millwrighting.

The result was a building so well designed and constructed that it continued to function perfectly as an aircraft production plant almost a quarter of a century later, serving actively throughout World War II. The building—some twenty-eight acres under one roof—stretched over an area equivalent to eight or ten city blocks. Completed in only ninety working days—thirty days ahead of schedule—it remained for many years the largest factory building

Samuel Austin planting a "second-line trench" of potatoes at his Willoughby, Ohio, home, 1918.

in the world and a unique instance of early twentieth-century high wide-span construction.

"A Vision Fulfilled" That this achievement must have been a personal triumph for Samuel Austin as he reached nearly half a century in his adopted nation, may be seen in an unusual advertisement that appeared in the pages of *The Literary Digest* and *The Saturday Evening Post* late in 1918 as the war was drawing swiftly to a close. In it, a handsomely limned and white-haired Samuel Austin (his first and only presence in an Austin ad) sits before a drafting table and draws a standard factory building. From the plans before him, the steel skeleton of an enormous building rises mysteriously and majestically. It stretches across the page to the vast open space on the opposite leaf, where sections of the building stand virtually complete. Hundreds of men, dwarfed by the structure, work swiftly, diligently, beneath the shadow of the massive beams. It is a vision of engineering strength emerging literally from the pen of experience. And, if it is fanciful—Samuel Austin was *not* an engineer—we can easily excuse it. The panoramic dream-like drawing represents (a headline tells us) A VISION FULFILLED. And the building is, of course, the Curtiss aircraft plant—as vital and as modern as the aeroplanes within. Through the almost poetic shorthand in which forty years of history have been condensed, the largest enclosed structure in the world is shown to have evolved directly from the hand of Samuel Austin. Even in the present age of cynicism, it is a very moving ad.

Aftermath of War Advertising continues to be done on a national scale and at a large expenditure. We are the best known industrial construction company in the country today—and abroad we are not unknown—because *The Saturday Evening Post* and *Literary Digest* have a large foreign circulation, and we have received many foreign inquiries as a direct result.

Extensive Advertising So reported the secretary of The Austin Company to the board of directors shortly after the signing of the armistice at Compiègne in November, 1918. With the mails bringing scores of inquiries daily from a widespread business community increasingly curious about the Austin Method and the utility of standard buildings, and with a growing number of handsomely illustrated brochures and booklets designed specifically to illustrate their advantages and benefits, the company was well launched in an area in which it had pioneered: industrial advertising. If Austin was the first engineering-construction firm to advertise on a consistent basis, then *consistency* would seem to have been the watchword of its advertising policy from the start. From the selection of Fuller & Smith as its agency shortly before the First World War to any forthcoming *Fortune* ad placed by Fuller & Smith & Ross today, Austin's graphic design, in particular, has been consistently in advance of its time, as has been the quality of its copy. Both reflect a high regard for the industries and institutions that the company seeks to attract. And both provide a consistent and comforting reminder, perhaps, that designers of well-constructed buildings are the first to recognize their kinship with designers of another sort: those who build with words and illustrations.

But at its inception not everyone was quite so serious or high-minded about Austin's advertising program. Although it surely contributed considerably to the company's entry into almost every branch of modern industry, the average Austin employee, privy to the contents of some of the letters received by the advertising department, saw a lighter side of the story:

"Results"

Gentlemen:

I am interested in buildings and am a carpenter by trade; in looking over the *Saturday Evening Post*, I was attracted by one of your large advertisements.

You state in the captions at the head, "A better use of Men. A better use of Time," but there is that in the illustration which negatives much of the force of your statements. The scaffold in the illustration is very poorly constructed. In use it would be dangerous for the men and wasteful of time; it is a very simple thing to construct a proper scaffold. Time and experience have established the soundness of this fact. Notice the scattering haphazard braces; these should run continuous from the ground to the top of the scaffold; and as nearly as possible to an angle of forty-five degrees. I will not elaborate further and trust you will pardon me in calling your attention to this rather glaring discrepancy.

Letters like this one, received in 1919, were a regular feature of *Results*, a short-lived in-house newsletter that, with the hindsight of the present, provides a welcome footnote to the past. The all-too-few surviving issues of *Results* reveal the human presence behind the nameless faces that were then designing and constructing some of the largest and most modern industrial buildings in the world. At its best it is witty and incisive; poetry abounds— some of it quite good—and it is rich in the laughter and camaraderie of men at work. It also breaks down the hoary, but persistent, stereotype of the American engineer as a man in baggy tweeds and white cotton socks, who loves his slide rule more than his wife. *Results*, among other things, is a repository of the courting habits of the American male, circa 1919–1920. The Austins may have frowned on alcohol, but they certainly had nothing against romantic love.

As to the Seattle carpenter whose letter is quoted above, he received an appreciative letter from his fellow craftsman, Mr. Samuel Austin, and the offending advertisement was never run again. But the following one-line inquiry—"Referring to your advertisement of October 13th [1919], will you kindly tell us how to find out the number of square feet that will be required in a building 50' x 100'?"—this, presumably, received no response at all.

Railroad Work

At the same 1918 board meeting mentioned earlier, the corporate secretary reported that "the railroad department, begun in 1917, continues to function well, and we have just received twelve new contracts. . . ." Austin's first major post-war area of concentration, the nation's railways, was a logical choice, indicative in every way of the conservative, but deliberate pattern of growth that had been in evidence from the company's start. In a sense, Austin has survived where so many others have failed because it has *good eyes:* that is, it is quick to spot new areas of growth or old ones that require technological transfusion. If it can competently provide a service sorely needed by industry—new or old—it is unhesitatingly aggressive in offering its services. The railroad industry is a case in point.

By the time of World War I, railroads in North America had for the most part reached the end of their great period of extensive development. Since the networks were largely laid down, new

Promoting the Austin Method, 1925.

construction slowed and a period of intensive development in the more densely populated and industrialized areas of the nation began. Although single-track lines were converted into double track, and double track in some cases to triple or quadruple track, much of the added capacity required to meet the transport needs of the twentieth century had to be provided by increasing the load-hauling ability of trains and by increasing their frequency over given segments. Trains were going to have to be both heavier and longer.

Realizing that these technological changes would necessitate, among other things, the installation of longer turntables and the enlargement of engine houses—not to mention the construction of plants in which to build new superheated engines—Austin moved with dispatch to offer its services. Eventually, once the level of business justified the move, it extended its program of standardization to cover the special needs of the railroad industry. By 1918, only one year after its railroad division had been established, Austin was offering a complete line of standard railway buildings, including roundhouses (20 stalls in 90 working days), locomotive erecting and machine shops (500 linear feet in 120 working days), freight car repair shops (600 linear feet in 60 working days), and many other standard units. It offered, as well, a complete railroad terminal program in which it could undertake the studies for passenger, freight, and engine terminal layouts and then design and construct them in record time.

Diversification

And so it went throughout the '10s and '20s, in industry after industry. Austin supplied whatever engineering services were available within the areas of its technological expertise. And where it lacked such expertise, it took the necessary steps to correct its shortcoming.

Take the automobile, for example. Austin designed and constructed everything from the plants that built it and the refineries that fueled it to the garages and stations that housed and serviced it. And then there were laundries and dry-cleaning plants. New technology had recently replaced the scrubboard, and an entire industry had to be rebuilt from scratch and housed in quarters that could accommodate the new machinery. And of course there were potteries, chemical plants, confectioneries, fertilizer manufactures, food processing plants, foundries and forge shops, glass plants, machine shops, mining facilities, paper mills, printing plants, power houses, steel works, dry docks, textile mills, aircraft plants and hangars, tractor factories—to mention just a few. Even that famous nineteenth-century cooperative of handicraftsmen, the Oneida Community, was completely overhauled by Austin in the 1920s.

But mindful of its origins, The Austin Company did not confine itself to the world of industry alone, and continued throughout the '20s to craft fine houses—as well as hospitals and theaters, hotels and country clubs, colleges and schools, shops and department stores, bus terminals and airports. Not even the "cities of the silent" were untouched by Austin versatility, the company having once designed and built one of the most fashionable mausoleums in Hollywood.

Thus, by 1924, Austin's list of clients had become a veritable index of the state of business in America, a catalogue of heft that indirectly echoed the nation's Indian-hatted president: The business of Austin is business.

Looking Forward At the beginning of 1924, Samuel Austin, then 73, retired from the presidency of the company he had founded and was in turn succeeded by his son. Had he chosen to look back upon the past forty-six years, he would have seen the transformation of his tiny carpentry shop at 4401 Broadway into a national network of decentralized district offices. Had he chosen to look back, he would have witnessed the slow development of the Austin Method into a comprehensive building service that brought together all the facilities of building—from site selection to the design and installation of equipment—under the roof of a single organization. But, God-fearing man that he was, and mindful of the fate of Lot's wife, he chose instead to look ahead. The future of the company lay not only in the hands of his son, but in those of the Austin staff as well. Thus he left the presidency secure in the knowledge that the company no longer belonged exclusively to him or to his family. Since 1914, as an incentive to continued excellence, key members of the staff had had the opportunity to buy stock in the company, an opportunity that would be expanded in the future.

Aviation During the period of rapid industrial expansion in the late '20s, the Austin organization pioneered on many other fronts as well. Wilbert Austin's contacts with the country's largest aircraft manufacturers had convinced him of the need for improved hangar doors. The original canopy door for wide-span hangars was developed under his guidance. It was the prototype of many to follow and aided the company in establishing leadership in the design and construction of airports and other air transport facilities.

Wilbert Austin's first love, in fact, was aviation. Some of his visionary ideas about air terminals published in popular magazine articles are only now coming into being, more than fifty years after they were first proposed. Significantly, under his aegis and after Lindbergh's historic flight the Austin logotype—the symbol familiarly known as "the pretzel" ever since its inception—underwent a change in design that caught the very spirit of the late '20s: it sprouted wings.

The New Era In the fall of 1929, with business booming and the future bright, the managers and directors of The Austin Company convened at a formal dinner in a Cleveland hotel. They were celebrating the start of a sales and marketing campaign called "The New Era" that reflected not only the approaching start of a new decade, but all the excitement and vitality that the year 1930 seemed to suggest. Work was then nearing completion on Burbank's United Airport, the nation's most modern terminal. This was surely the start of a new era, an era of unprecedented speed in which the triumph of the airplane was the ultimate triumph of the machine. And Austin was prepared to continue to create and to innovate in this new era soon to come.

And, so, contemporary photographs show a group of men in dinner jackets and slicked-down patent-leather hair, engineers and architects and technologists all. Some hold cigars. A few grin into the camera's lens. Overhead flutter the streamers and banners gaily proclaiming THE NEW ERA.

The next week the bottom dropped out of the stock market.

Examples of Austin Standard Daylight Buildings "for all industries—from lamps to locomotives." *Right:* No. 1 with monitor—"ideal for light manufacturing." *Below:* No. 3 (originally No. 103)—the "Universal Type—ideal because of its wide areas of unobstructed floor space." *Opposite (above):* "Steelspan" garage employing Austin's clear-span steel truss; *(middle):* No. 4, a sawtooth building for "any manufacturing process requiring well-diffused light"; *(below):* No. 9, a multi-story structure of reinforced concrete.

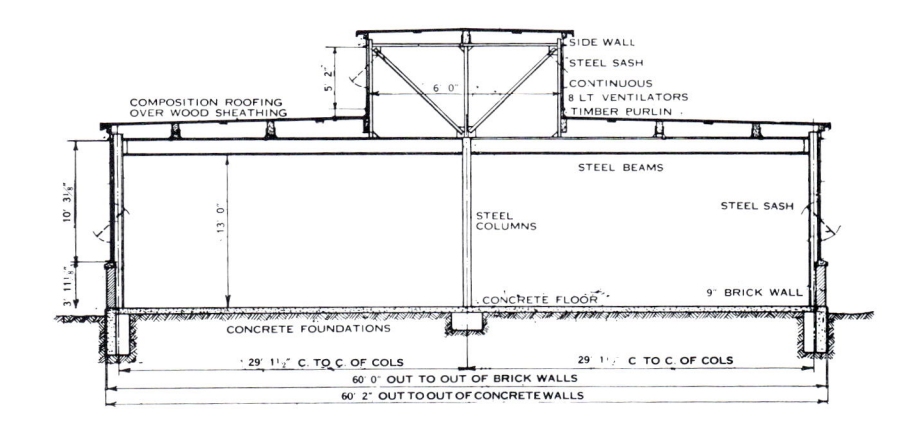

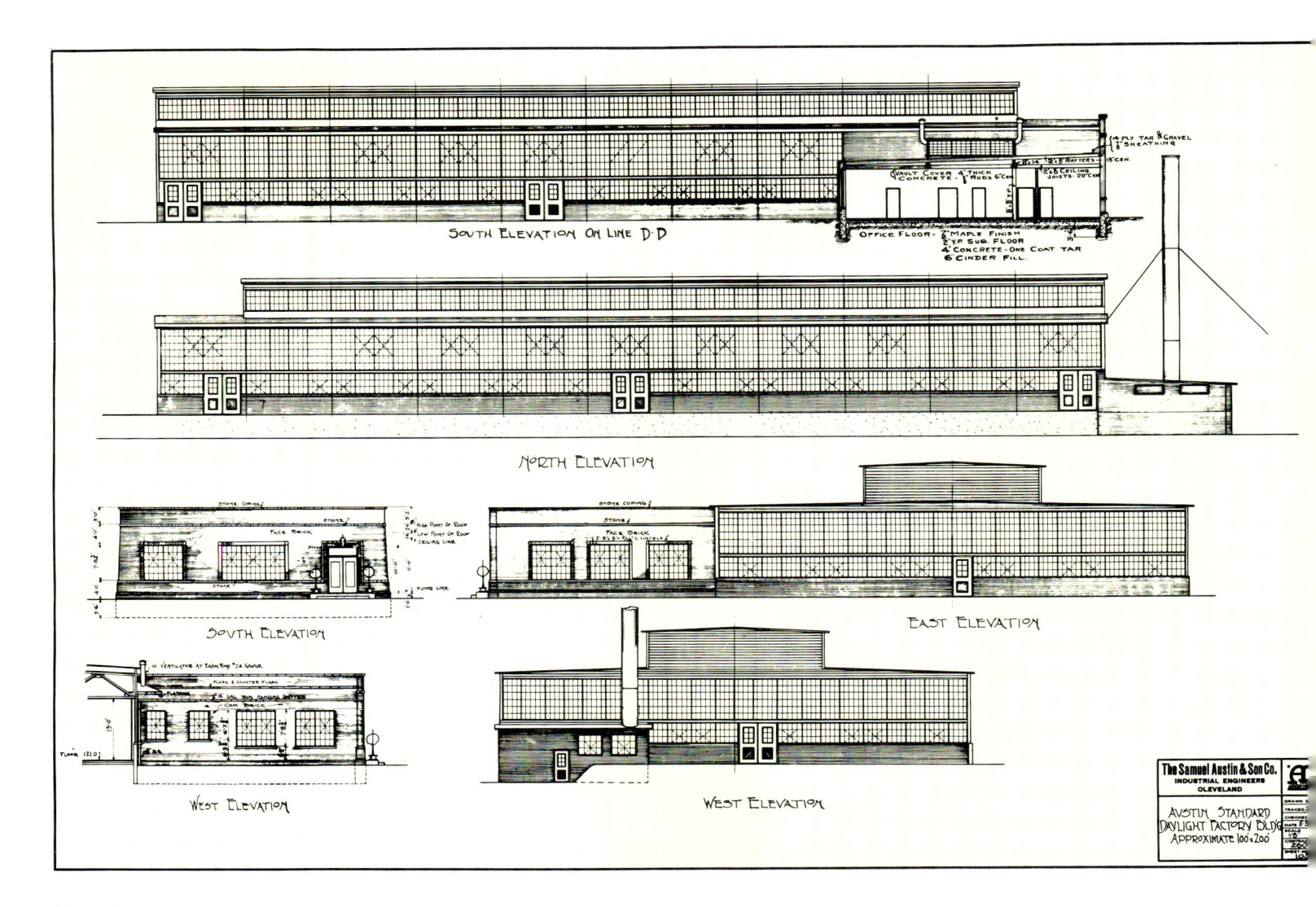

A New Austin Standard Building

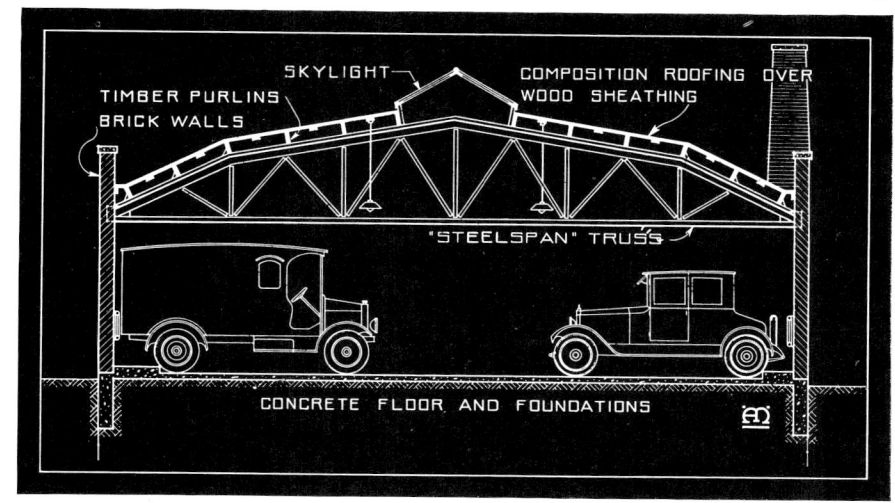

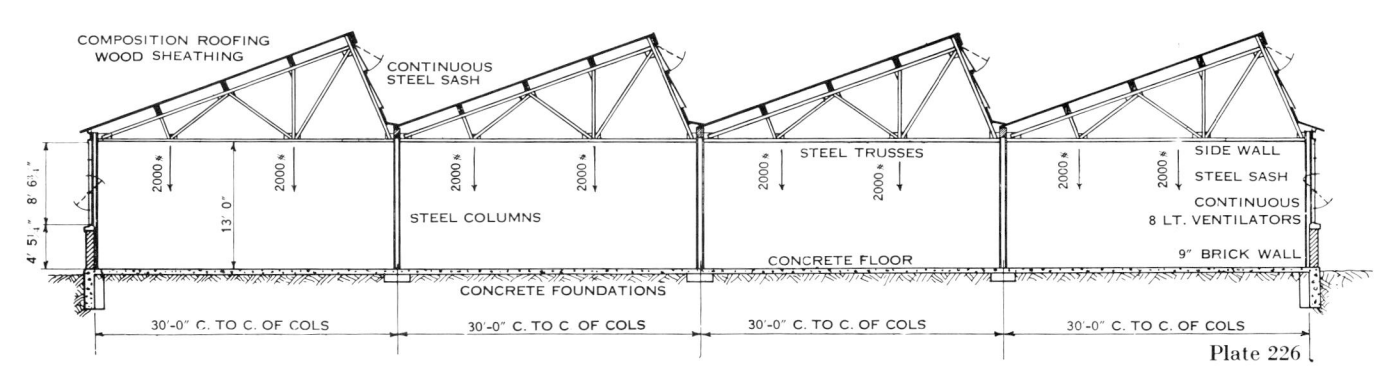

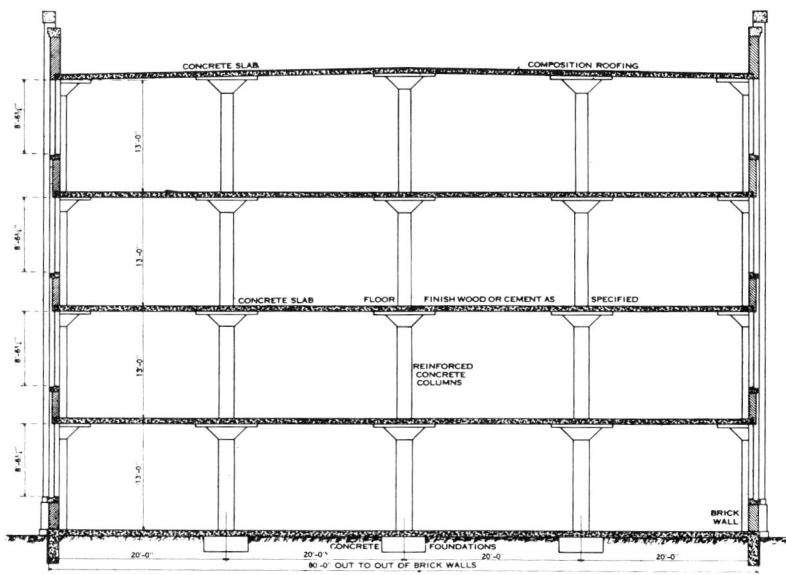

In an advertisement that appeared nationally in *The Saturday Evening Post* in the spring of 1918, The Austin Company presented the "Log of an Industrial Building," a series of photographs showing the complete construction of a standard factory building for the National Cash Register Company of Dayton, Ohio, in 30 working days—from March 16th to April 25th—graphic proof that "Austin Means Speed."

71

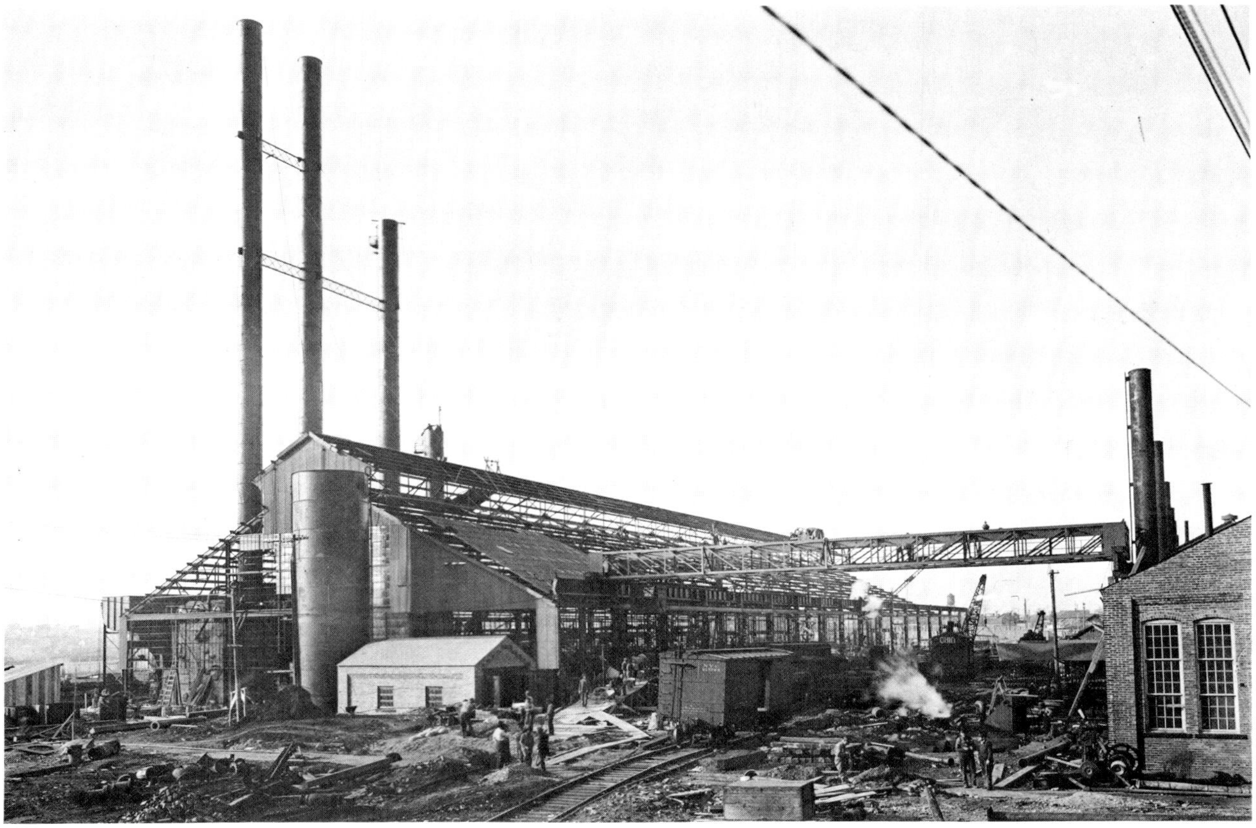

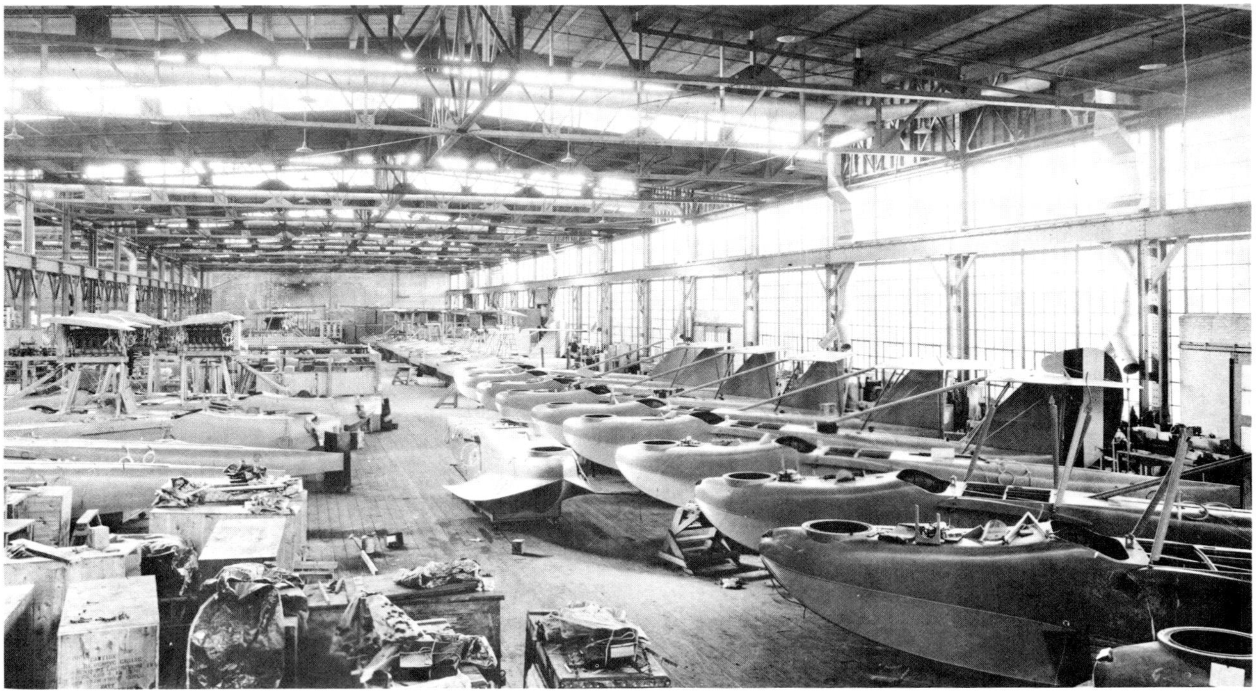

Austin's reputation for quality and speed made it an integral part of America's mobilization for war. *Opposite (above)*: One of many buildings constructed at the Frankford Arsenal, Philadelphia, Pennsylvania (1916). *Opposite (below)*: An interior view of the 28-acre aircraft plant designed and built for the Curtiss Aeroplane Company, Buffalo, New York (1918). *Above:* Erecting the Naval Aircraft factory at the Philadelphia Navy Yard (1917). *Below:* One of four radio towers under construction for the Navy Department at Annapolis, Maryland. The Navy radio station, which cost $1.5 million, was opened in 1918 by the Secretary of the Navy who sent radio greetings to London, Paris, and Rome.

Although Austin undertook international work as early as 1913, standardization increased the number of such projects. *Below:* Dominion Steel Co., Brantford, Ontario (1918); Cape Town (South Africa) Explosives Co. (1919); *Opposite:* Dominion Glass Co., Redcliff, Alberta (1913); Merlini S. A., Buenos Aires, Argentina (c. 1918); Dominion Chain Co., Niagara Falls, Ontario (1914).

75

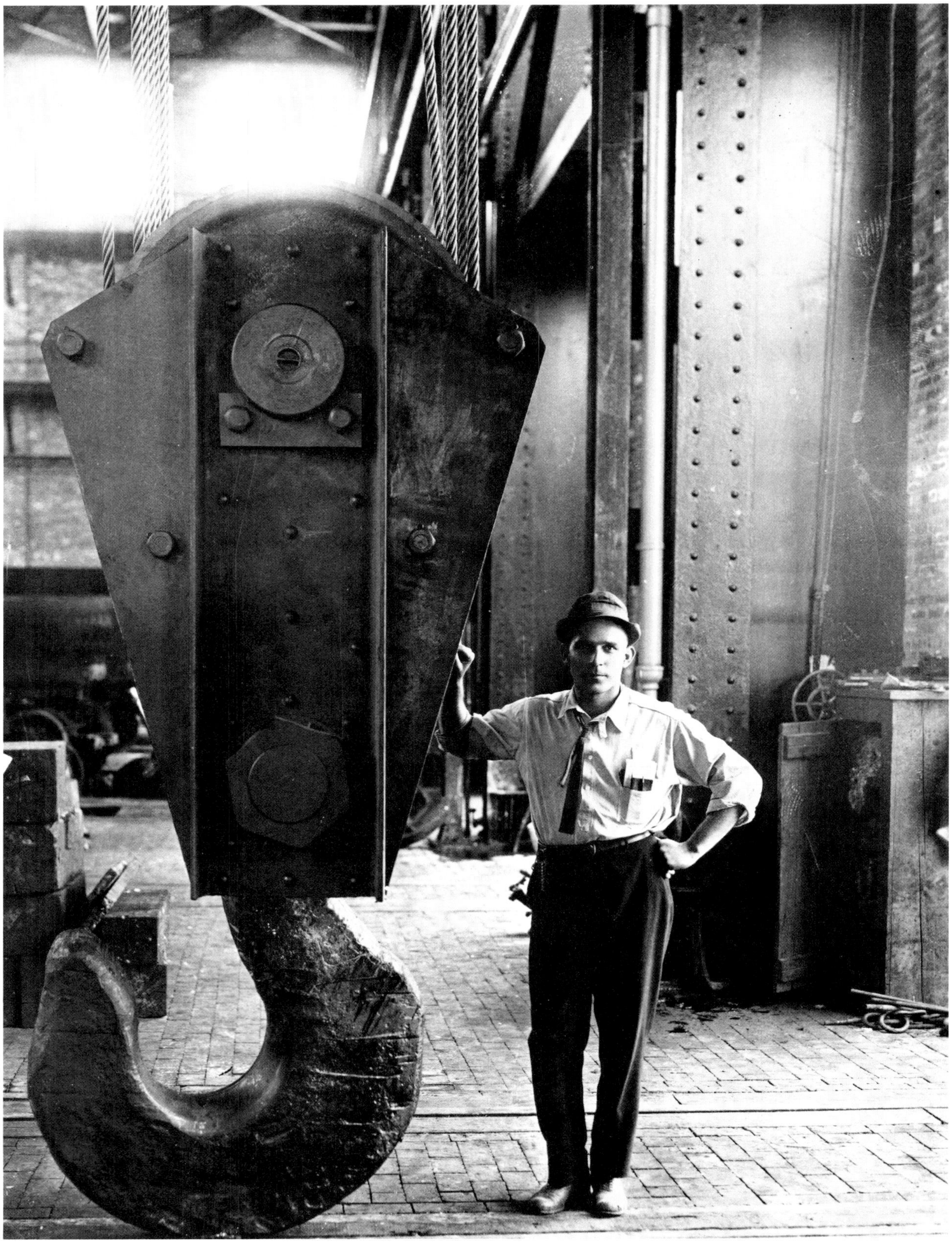

In 1917 Austin applied its successful program of standardization to buildings required by the railroad industry, including machine shops, locomotive erecting plants, freight car repair shops, roundhouses, and engine terminals. Within a year, contracts had been signed with 12 major lines. These illustrations are of the Pennsylvania R. R. erecting shop (1919) at Logansport, Indiana. The main erecting aisle, *below*, contained 17 pits and featured an upper crane runway, 46 feet high, that supported a 250-ton double trolley traveling crane, *opposite*, capable of lifting the world's largest locomotives. On the lower runway is a 10-ton crane for lighter work.

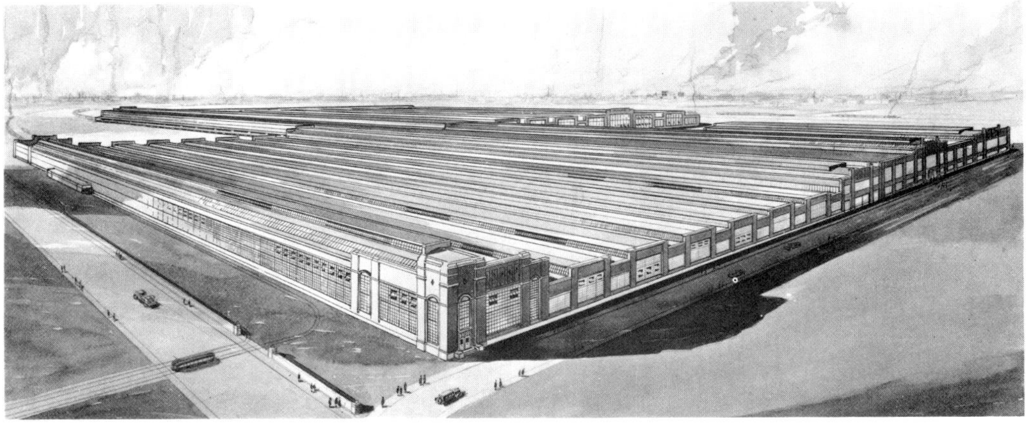

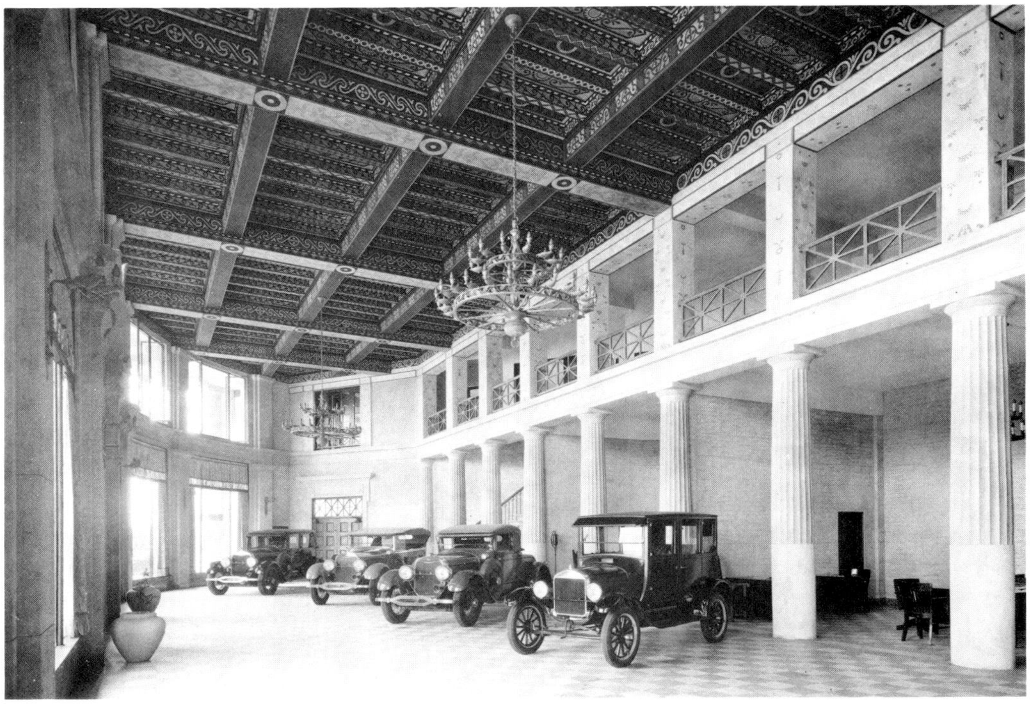

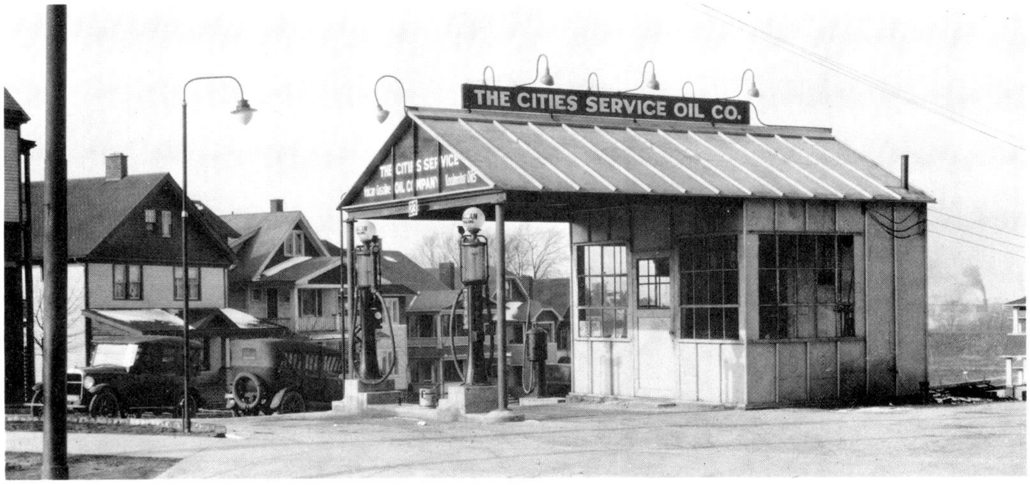
THE CITIES SERVICE OIL CO.

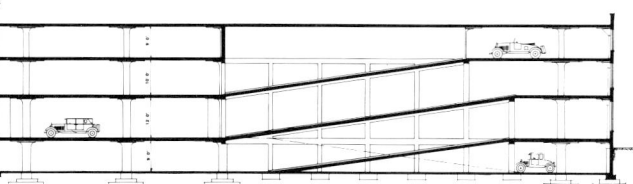

From the earliest days of the industry, Austin contributed to the burgeoning development of the automobile. These few illustrations only hint at the large number of projects undertaken in the '20s for the automotive industry. *Opposite:* The 35-acre Pontiac plant—then the world's largest—for the Oakland Motor Car Co., Pontiac, Michigan (1927); elaborate showroom of the S. A. Ryan Motor Co., Miami, Florida (1926); early filling station, Cleveland, Ohio (1920). *Above:* The Austin Ramp Garage, first built in 1924 and still a fundamental design of urban garages; a detail of the Pontiac plant assembly building. *Right:* Demonstrating the strength of a Steelspan truss in a Cleveland garage (1919).

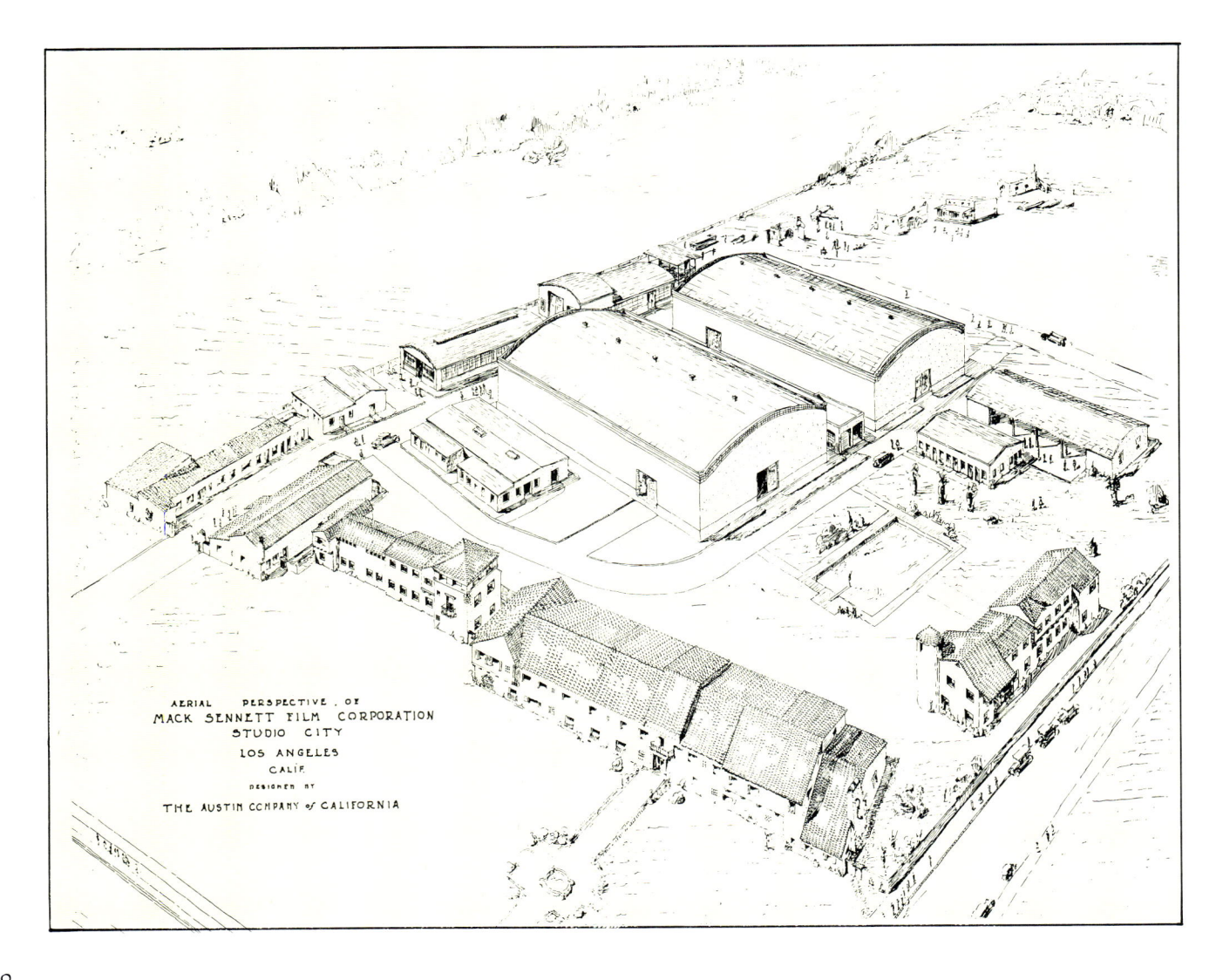

Main Building 700 Feet Long
Approximately
3 Acres of Floor Space

AERIAL PERSPECTIVE OF
MACK SENNETT FILM CORPORATION
STUDIO CITY
LOS ANGELES
CALIF.
DESIGNED BY
THE AUSTIN COMPANY OF CALIFORNIA

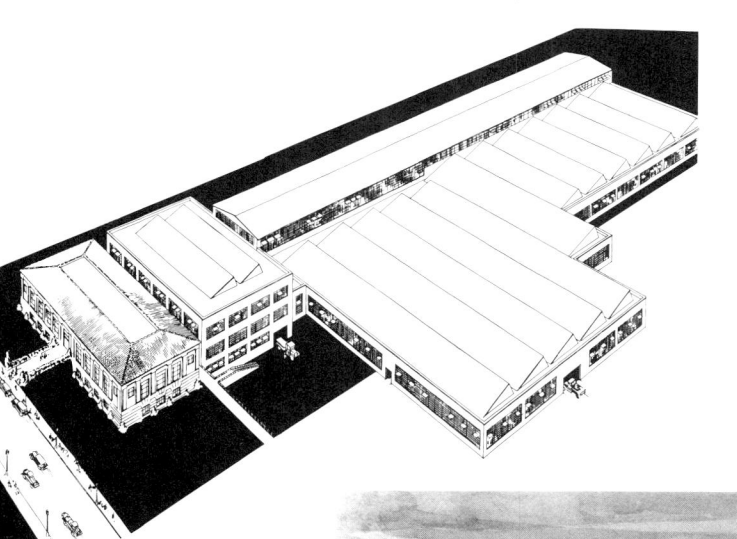

The variety of Austin projects in the '10s and '20s is evident in the contemporary renderings shown here and on the following two pages. *Opposite:* Torbenson Gear and Axle Co., Cleveland, Ohio (1916); Studio City, including two sound stages, for Mack Sennett Film Corporation, Hollywood, California (1927). *Above:* 16 plant units for Caterpillar Tractor Co., Peoria, Illinois (1929). *Left:* West Coast plant of Link-Belt Co., San Francisco, California (1929). *Below:* Johnson Motor Co. outboard motor plant, Waukegan, Illinois (1927).

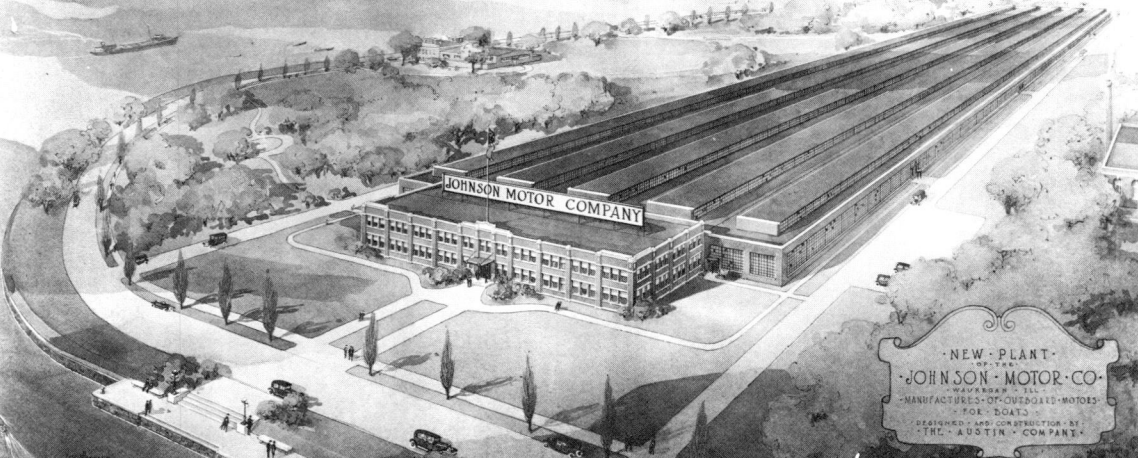

Above: The Mentor Harbor Yacht Club, Mentor, Ohio (1930). *Left:* Cadillac Combined Foundries, Cadillac Motor Car Co. (1925). *Below:* Ohio Bell Telephone Co., Cleveland, Ohio (1929). *Opposite:* The Du Bois Press, Rochester, New York (1926); Palmer House Hotel Laundry, Chicago, Illinois (1926).

83

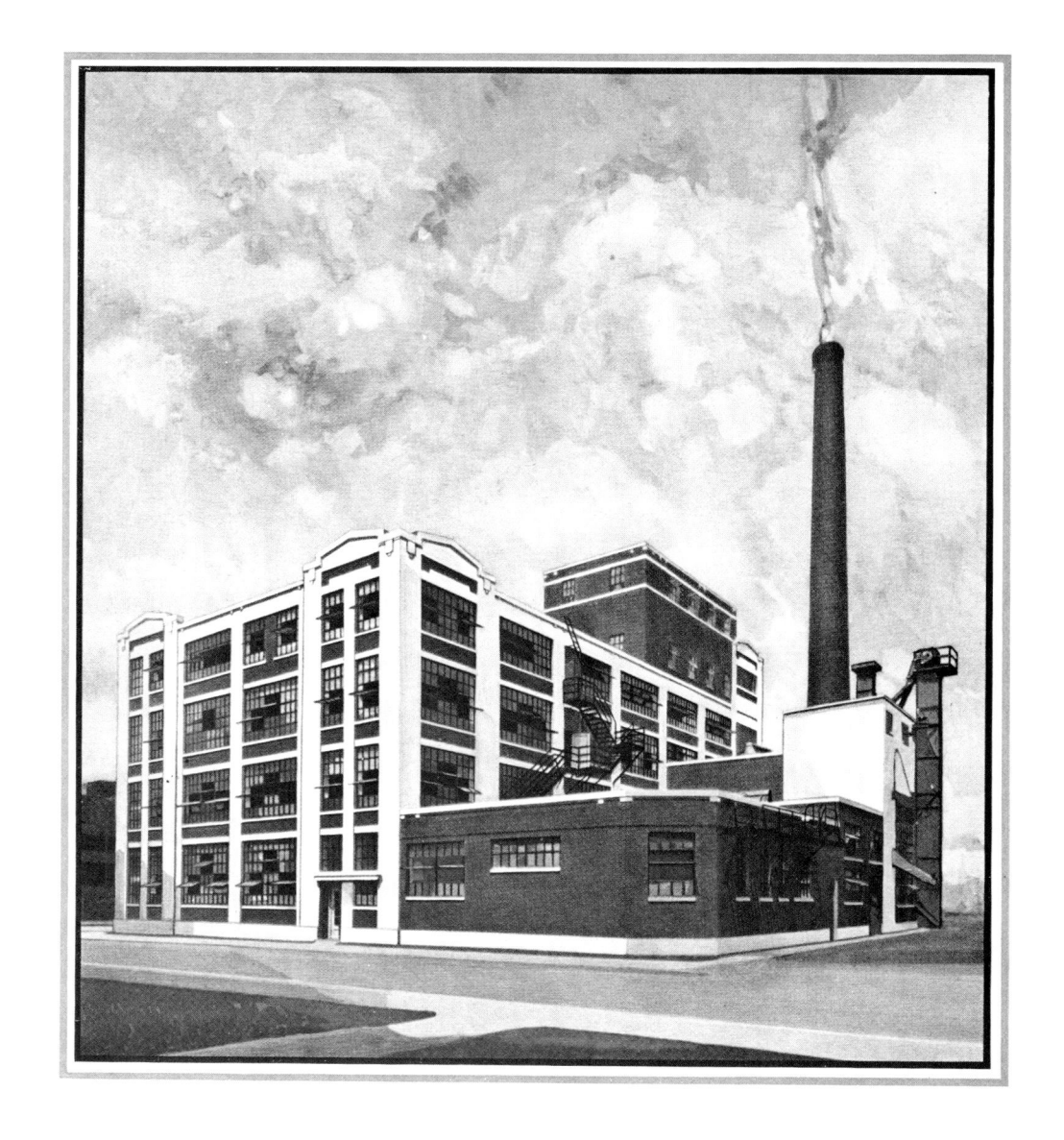

STORE & LOFT BUILDING SEATTLE WASH THE AUSTIN CO

S. H. KRESS & CO. 5-10-25 CENT STORE

BUILDING FOR E J HUSTON & M E SWANSTROM SEATTLE WASH THE AUSTIN CO SEATTLE WASH

Although the 1920s found Austin vigorously promoting the single-story industrial plant, it continued as one of the nation's prime designers and builders of downtown commercial structures. *Opposite:* Cheasty's Department Store, Seattle, Washington (1926–1927); one of many branch stores for S. H. Kress & Co., this one in Tacoma, Washington (1926); commercial building, Seattle, Washington (1925). *Above:* Commercial row, Beverly Hills, California (1927). *Right:* Nu-Art Engraving Co., Chicago, Illinois (1928).

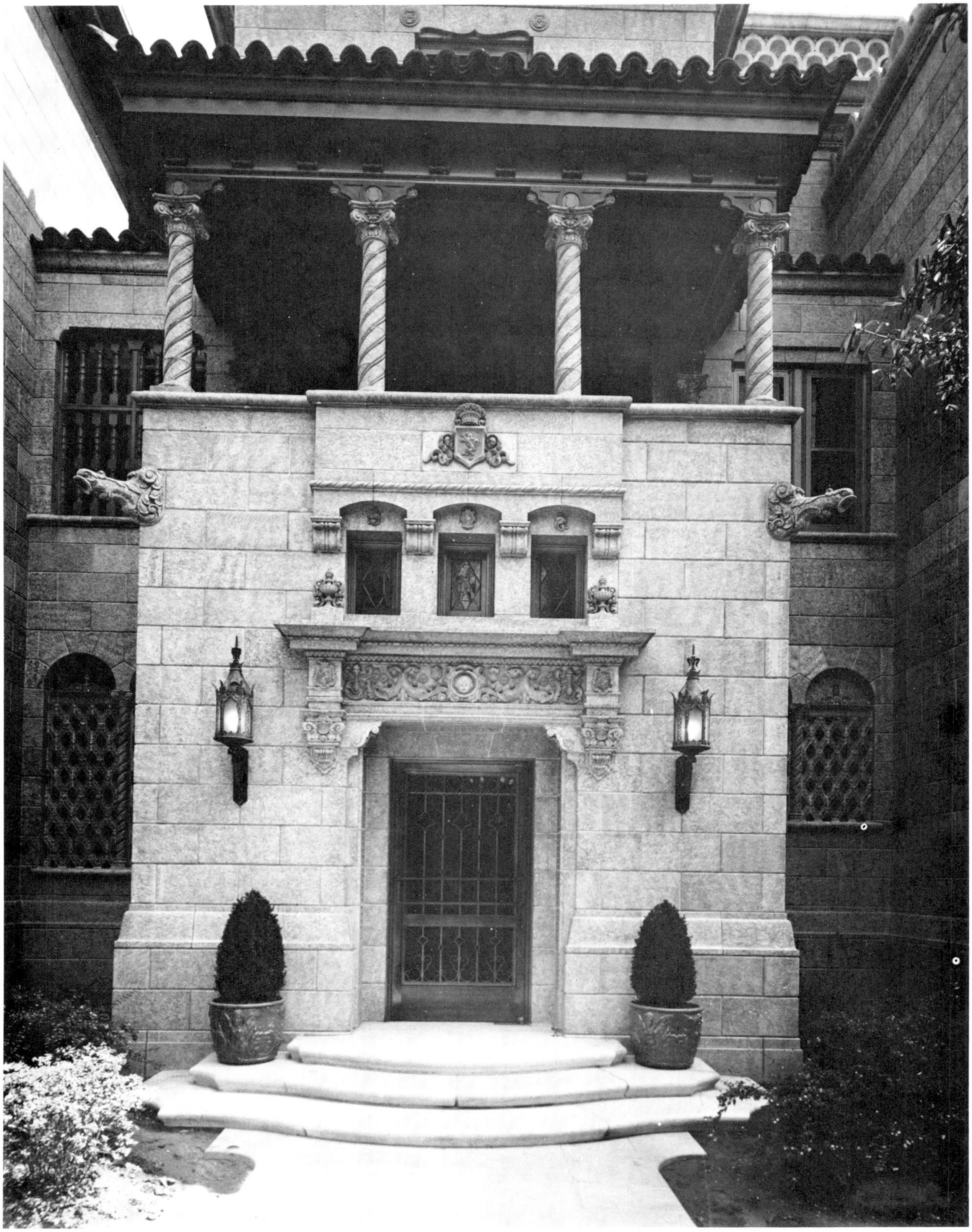

In the late '20s Austin excelled in building structures in the popular Spanish Mission style. *Opposite:* Mildred Apartments, Beaumont, Texas (1929). *Above:* Exterior and offices, Mars Incorporated plant, Chicago, Illinois (1928). *Below:* Private residence, Coral Gables, Florida (1928).

87

For at least a decade before the feats of Lindbergh and others made the public air-minded, Austin was actively designing and building hangars, aircraft factories, wind tunnels, and airports. By the late '20s, the company maintained its own airplane which sported the Austin "pretzel" as its insignia. *Above:* The Austin cantilever hangar with "Clear-Open" canopy doors at the Cleveland Airport (1929). *Right:* Interior of wind tunnel building of the National Advisory Committee for Aeronautics, Langley Field, Virginia (1925). *Below:* Wilbert J. Austin's design for an air terminal (1928); safety of passengers and protection from elements were to be assured by means of an underground tunnel to "ship stations."

Top (left): The original caption of this 1928 rendering read: "Providing speed, safety, and comfort for the air passengers. Air-Rail-Water-Highway Terminal of Austin design." *Top (right)* and *above*: Dirigible hangars built for the Goodyear Zeppelin Corporation at Wheeling, West Virginia, and at Round Hill, Massachusetts (1929).

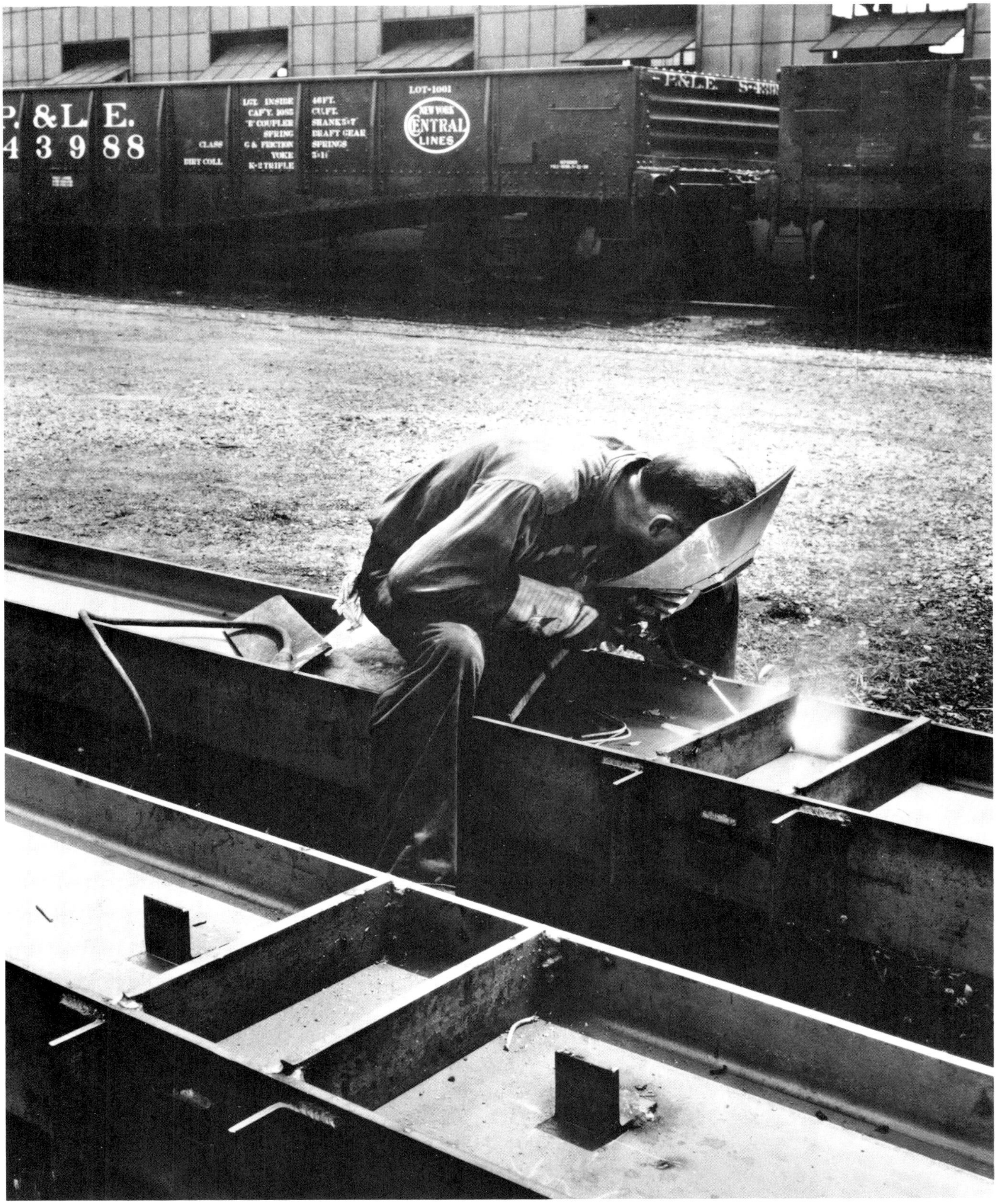
P. & L. E.
43988
LOT-1001
NEW YORK
CENTRAL
LINES

Having tested a riveted and a welded truss to destruction in 1925, Austin designed and built at its own expense a four-story and basement commercial building, *opposite* and *above*, in Cleveland in 1929 in order to try welding on a broader scale. As an experiment, no bolts or rivets were used, an approach that proved too extreme as much shoring was required to hold members in place before tack welding. *Right:* In all the nostalgic tributes paid to the 1876 Centennial Exposition during the recent Bicentennial celebration, virtually every historian forgot the lavish Sesquicentennial Exposition held in Philadelphia in 1926. Most of the Sesquicentennial buildings were designed and built by The Austin Company.

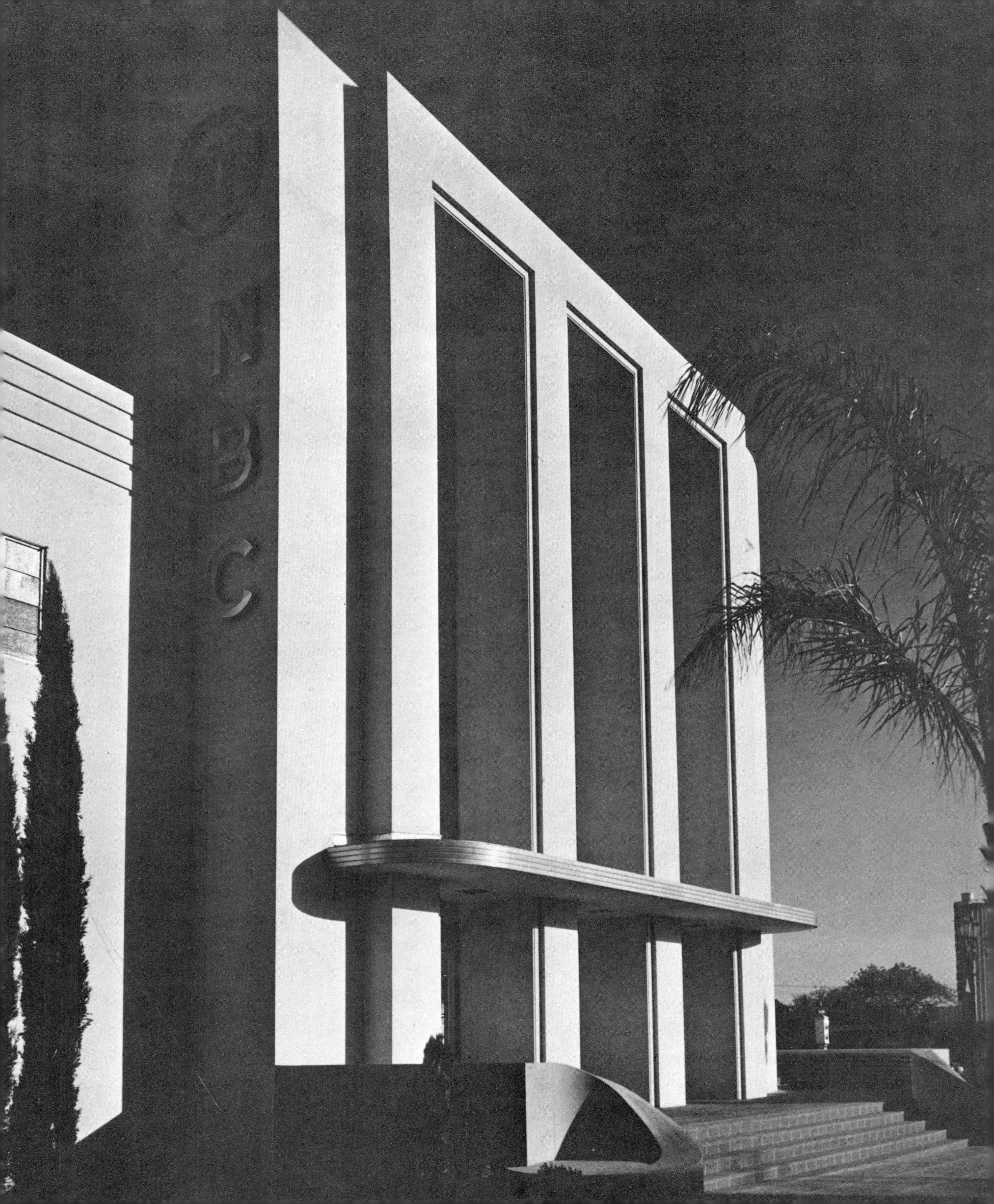
NBC

III The New Era: Austin in the '30s

The Early Days of the Depression

In the opening days of the new decade, the secretary of The Austin Company addressed the sober-faced members of the board of directors with a report on the "Business Outlook for 1930": "The effect of the stock market crash the last of October," he began, "was felt by us immediately, and our volume of sales for November, December, and January to date has been less than one-fourth of our volume preceding that time. The seriousness of the situation cannot be overlooked." Then, with a note of grim irony that must have cut to the very bone of the directors, he added: "Our New Era convention was most opportunely timed. . . ."

So this was the New Era: the entire American economy had sunk in a sea of despair by the beginning of 1930. And the bottom was still almost three years away. Consumer spending had already declined sharply, and the public, leery of banks, began to cache currency in safe-deposit boxes and in mattresses. Within three months of the Crash, every kind of business had suffered badly and had begun to discharge employees in increasing and alarming numbers. Workers, unable to find other jobs, defaulted on installment payments—worsening, in turn, an already crippled economy—and exhausted their savings in order to survive the long months ahead. In the larger cities the first breadlines were beginning to form. And, at the end of the third decade of the twentieth century, America, unlike England, had neither social security nor unemployment insurance to fall back on in hard times. All it had was a rapidly diminishing hope—and the fatuous words of its leaders.

In the face of this economic disaster, and with no other solution at hand, President Hoover became the voice of optimism itself: "Any lack of confidence in the basic strength of business is foolish," he said in November 1929. And two months later he reported that "Business and industry have turned the corner." "We have now passed the worst," he announced on May 1. And then, on June 28, 1930, when wheat had dropped in six months from $1.04 to 68 cents a bushel—and would go to 38 cents—and cotton had dropped from 19 cents to 13 cents a pound—and would go to 6.5 cents—James J. Davis, secretary of labor, attempted to assuage an anxious business community with these words: "Courage and resource are already swinging us back on the road to recovery. And we are fortunate in having a president who sets us

Opposite: The NBC Radio City of the West, Hollywood, California, 1938.

a shining example of that courage and initiative." The president, after all, had just summoned to the White House a troop of Girl Scouts who had shown him and Mrs. Hoover (and a small army of newsmen) how to prepare a nourishing meal for a family of six for less than a dollar. A shining example, all right.

Just as The National Association of Manufacturers began covering billboards with a poster designed by Howard Chandler Christy in which a Marcel-waved Columbia announced that "Business is Good. Keep it Good. Nothing can stop us," the directors of The Austin Company, knowing better, were already preparing for the worst. The building business had always been an accurate barometer of the state of the economy—and the mercury was dropping rapidly.

The First Issue of Fortune

The irony of the situation on that cold January day was underscored by the appearance of a new magazine a few days later. On the eve of the stock market collapse five months earlier, George A. Bryant, who was then executive vice president of the company, had been brought a dummy of a forthcoming magazine by the Cleveland manager of Time Inc., and, impressed by both layout and editorial content, had enthusiastically signed an advertising contract. Now, in February 1930, that advertisement—designed and placed in headier days—was making its first appearance. "A New Era in Industrial Building," its headline proclaimed above the outstretched wings of the "improved" Austin logotype. "FORTUNE Magazine inaugurates a new era in publishing. AUSTIN inaugurates a new era in design and construction of industrial plants."

February 1930 was not exactly the most propitious time to launch a new business magazine. Nor was it the ideal setting for a new era in industrial building. But, in spite of the Depression—and perhaps because of it—both notions were soon to be proved successful. A New Era had indeed arrived.

Two Landmarks

Fortunately for the men of Austin, the company had a sufficient backlog of work to make it through the first two years of the Great Depression. Two of these projects, in fact, became landmarks in the history of the company, although for two entirely different reasons. Both had their origins in the prosperous days before the Crash, and both must be viewed within the total picture of the company's rapidly developing engineering technology. The first of these projects was the creation of the world's first "controlled conditions" plant. The second was the design and construction of an entire Russian city, intended by Joseph Stalin to be the first Soviet industrial utopia. Both had been conceived and executed by Austin.

Evolution of the Controlled Conditions Plant

Innovation at The Austin Company, as elsewhere, develops not so much as a result of spontaneous inspiration, but as a logical progression from earlier innovation. Work on incandescent lamp factories, as we have seen, led both to the refinement of the Austin Method and to the introduction of standardized steel-frame industrial buildings. Then the company built its own fabricating plant to furnish its steelwork more promptly, and this consequently reduced the time for completing industrial projects, thus setting a vigorous pace for industrial construction and putting new meaning into "bonus and penalty" clauses. The perfection of standardized one-story buildings—particularly of the daylight building, in which the pilasters were eliminated and the sash had an uninterrupted run—led, in turn, to still another corollary of the Austin Method: the vigorous presentation of the case for single-story industrial buildings as the most inexpensive and efficient means of housing industrial production. Austin's advocacy of the single-story plant, perhaps more than any other development of its early history, changed the industrial skyline of America and, by the late 1920s, had gained almost universal acceptance.

In the mid-1920s, Austin borrowed an innovative leaf from other engineers—the principle of welding—and turned it to its own advantage. As early as 1925, it had welded the structural members for one bay in a large 50-ton crane runway at the Pittsburgh Transformer Company plant, which was otherwise of conventional riveted construction. And, in 1929, it had decided to invest a substantial sum in the construction of a 4-story office building in Cleveland. This—the first all-welded commercial structure in America—was undertaken for the engineering experience it would afford, and was constructed entirely at the company's expense. Austin's years of costly experimentation and research in advancing welding had, in fact, precipitated the promotional theme of the ill-timed New Era convention. In late 1929, it had publicly an-

Austin's first *Fortune* advertisement, February 1930.

95

nounced its new service in welded steel construction as "the beginning of a new era in the building art," at a cost comparable with the prevailing cost of other forms of construction.[1]

And now, in 1930, Austin was prepared to announce a new idea, a revolutionary one that followed logically from its successful experience with welding and from its years of experience in having perfected the one-story "straight-line" factory building. The controlled conditions plant owed its existence to both.

The Controlled Conditions Plant

In developing the controlled conditions plant, modern science was invoked for the first time to provide an ideal environment for factory workers. The theory was not entirely original to Austin, since the possibility of windowless buildings had been discussed by engineers for some years before Gifford K. Simonds, president of Simonds Industries (later the Simonds Saw and Steel Company), first approached The Austin Company in 1929 to develop an entirely new type of factory, entirely windowless, that depended completely for its light and ventilation on artificial sources. In fact, with the coming of talking pictures, a large movie studio in Germany had been constructed without windows in the late 1920s, an occurrence that may well have been known to Austin engineers since the company had only recently pioneered in the construction of the first large talking picture studios in Hollywood.

In planning the Simonds plant, every factor affecting the five senses of human beings was studied and analyzed by Austin engineers with the utmost scientific care. They aimed to create conditions that would be ideally comfortable for operatives and hence conducive to the greater efficiency of the plant itself. The complete interior environment of the plant, then, was to be mechanically controlled: an air-conditioning system was to supply a continuous flow of air, both recirculated and fresh, carefully regulated as to temperature, cleanliness, humidity, and rate of supply. Artificial lighting was to supply great, constant intensities where they were needed rather than to depend on daylight, which of course varies when clouds obscure the sun, when the sun rises or sets, in poor weather, and in different seasons. Heat and gases

---

[1] In March 1931, a supplementary announcement told of an even more surprising development—Austin was now offering noiseless welded construction at *less* cost than the riveted type.

generated in some manufacturing processes were to be drawn off mechanically and vented to the outside. The interior of the plant was to be acoustically treated to reduce reverberation and to confine noise to the immediate area in which it was produced. And the use of color was to be employed to demark the location of equipment.

In short, if this daring experiment succeeded—and the leaders of American industry were all watching intently—a New Era would indeed be born. By mid-1930, construction of the world's first controlled conditions plant was well under way.

Austin and the Soviet Workers' Utopia

At about the same time that Gifford Simonds was dreaming of a factory in which a sunny day in spring could be artificially reproduced throughout the year, another dreamer was devising plans of his own. In October 1928, Joseph Stalin announced his first Five-Year Plan, directed toward a mass industrialization of the Soviet Union. Revolutionary in the extreme and rigorously pressed upon the Russian people, the program was based upon the dictator's belief that the Soviet Union was "fifty to one hundred years behind the advanced countries" and "must cover this distance in ten years." And he was prepared to pay large amounts of Russian gold for the technical assistance of two American advisors most capable of helping him attain his goal: Henry Ford and The Austin Company.

Henry Ford had long been considered a Russian hero—not as a capitalist, of course, but as a true revolutionary who through the development of modern mass production had placed the luxury of the automobile within easy reach of the worker. More Russians, it was said, had heard of Henry Ford than had heard of Joseph Stalin—especially since some 85 percent of all the trucks and tractors and automobiles in Russia were Ford-made.

The Austin Company, although unknown to the average Russian, was very well known to the engineers upon whom Stalin depended for the successful execution of the *sine qua non* of his Five-Year Plan: the construction of an enormous automotive factory and workers' city. Austin, after all, had only recently (1927) designed and built the world's largest and most efficient automobile plant—the new Pontiac Six factory, a structure encompassing 35 acres of floor space that had been erected in only seven months' time. Within a month of its completion, General Motors had announced "Surprising price reductions—made possible by the efficiency and economies of the world's largest and finest motor car factory." Austin had just the requisite reputation for speed and efficiency that Stalin needed if Russian-made Model A's were to roll off the Soviet assembly line by 1932.

Early in 1929, the Supreme Economic Council of the Union of Socialist Soviet Republics created the state trust, Autostroy, to establish an automobile manufacturing industry with the capacity to produce 140,000 automobiles and trucks per year. It would be the largest automotive factory in Europe and would require, in addition, the construction of a complete workers' city that would ultimately house 50,000 people—complete with all such public utilities as water supply system, storm and sanitary sewer systems, central power and heating plant for both factory and city, electric power and light systems, telephones—in fact, everything required by the modern industrial community[2]

But, before Autostroy could attempt to secure the services of The Austin Company, it first had to obtain the cooperation of Henry Ford. By late spring, after long and complicated negotiations, an agreement was made with the Ford Company to permit Autostroy to use Ford plans, specifications, and methods—any reservations that Henry Ford might have had about doing business with the Russians having vanished after Autostroy strongly hinted that a deal with General Motors might be imminent. If Ford was not willing to offer help, then General Motors would. Ford signed on the dotted line.

---

[2] No definitive study of the Austin-designed-and-built Russian Ford plant at Nizhni Novgorod has yet been written, although the complete story would prove one of the most interesting chapters in the early history of American-Soviet relations. The most complete telling to date is Robert Scoon's "Those Communist Model A's" (*The Restorer*, March-April 1970), an informative and entertaining article that is nonetheless marred by many inaccuracies, particularly in those sections dealing with The Austin Company. It is difficult to trust a researcher who is not even certain of the company's correct name. Even less trustworthy is the section on Nizhni Novgorod in the recently published *The Brothers Reuther*.

The best contemporary observation is Allan S. Austin's "Communism Builds Its City of Utopia" (*The New York Times Magazine*, August 9, 1931), in which the then 26-year-old grandson of the founder of The Austin Company explores the sociological and political significance of this remarkable new city. The article, however, necessarily omits any discussion of events leading up to the model community's construction.

That summer, at the invitation of Autostroy engineers who had visited the Austin offices in Cleveland earlier in the year, George Bryant inspected the proposed site of the industrial utopia —a narrow tongue of land above the intersection of the Volga and Oka rivers, about eight miles northeast of the ancient city of Nizhni Novgorod. After long negotiations, during which Bryant operated from the Grand Hotel on Revolutionary Square in Moscow, communicating daily with Cleveland by wire, Austin was awarded the contract to design and supervise the construction of the entire project on August 23, 1929. The contract—amounting to some 60 million dollars—was the most substantial that the Soviet Union had initiated since the revolution in 1917.

Upon his return from Moscow aboard the *Berengaria*, Bryant was greeted by newsmen who immediately—and erroneously— reported that "the new city [would] be named 'Austingrad' in honor of the builders," an unfounded claim never considered seriously by the Russians or by The Austin Company.

A special commission of Russian engineers, working at the Ford plant in Dearborn, Michigan, and in collaboration with the engineers of The Ford Motor Company, provided The Austin Company with the general sizes and equipment data for the various auto plant buildings, from which Austin engineers prepared complete construction plans. The large automotive plant, modeled in part on the Ford plants at River Rouge and at Highland Park, was to cover an area of 600 acres, encompassing approximately 3 million square feet of floor space, including complete foundry, spring shop, forge shop, pressed steel shop, machine and assembly shop, power house, warehouses, trade school, etc. (The relative size of these buildings can be estimated from the dimensions of the largest, the machine and assembly building—1800 feet long by 350 feet wide.) All buildings were to be of the latest factory design, with steel or reinforced concrete frames, masonry and steel sash wall, insulated wood roofs, and wood block floors—and a modern system of reinforced concrete highways was to surround all buildings. Austin's construction plans were also to include all systems for plumbing, heating, ventilating, process piping, and sprinklers. Austin, in short, had agreed to a typical "complete service" contract. The difference, however, was that some 26,000 Russian workers—largely unskilled peasants and women—were to be involved—and on the native soil of a communistic nation not yet recognized by the government of the United States.

In April 1930, a specially appointed group of construction, mechanical, and electrical engineers was sent to Nizhni Novgorod to commence the actual construction of the project, and the cornerstone of the first building was laid on May 1, 1930. Shortly thereafter, the Austin engineers were joined by their Russian colleagues from the Ford plant at Dearborn, and, in the fall of that year, both engineering groups—American and Russian—were joined by still another group of Austin engineers who had been sent to redesign the mechanical and electrical equipment. The original plan, prepared in the Cleveland office, had called for using American-made pipe, fixtures, and other material. Now, the ever-worsening economic picture in America had rendered that plan useless. By mid-1930, the stock market continued to fall with increasing rapidity and did not reach bottom until the end of 1932.

From the beginning, the problems faced by the American engineers in executing their commission were formidable. In addition to extreme personal discomfort caused by life in this still-backward country, they encountered the stubborn resistance of the Russian peasants who had been assigned to them as laborers. An American visitor, touring the site in July 1931, noted that "building materials were dumped about without regard to where they were to be used," and that "twice as many workers were evident as would be required on a similar job in the United States, with twice as much time required to get it done. One American engineer for Austin, unable to speak a word of Russian, attempted to direct hod carriers to remove an excess number of bricks from a roof-top. The result of his sign language was that even more bricks were brought up to the roof." And then there was the problem of de-lousing 26,000 peasant workers.

The incredible frustration of all involved in this project—Americans and Russians alike—is brilliantly captured in a manuscript, written in vividly colorful broken-English, by one of the Russian engineers. Somehow it has been preserved through the years. In one poignant passage, he bitterly berates the negligent Russian bureaucrats for insufferable delays and gross inefficiency and for the wretched or nonexistent training given the peasant workers:

There are on the dock 15,000 tons of gravel, pyramids of sand, stone, cement, machines, lumber. Buildings cry out and demand all this. Have you thought about the plan of their delivery and transportation to the different districts? Every day workers on the dock receive new instructions from you. Every day you make people destroy and remake what was done yesterday. Valuable summer days pass and you sigh softly while young Communists from all districts are carrying the gravel on their shoulders; while the movable conveyors rust in storage; while a misplaced pump is being carried from one place to another because you did not clearly indicate its proper place; while an expensive crane, which can replace the work of 200 workers, stands unassembled on the dock because there was nobody who could be spared to assemble it when it arrived; while tons of concrete was mixed—by hand—even though a mechanical concrete mixer stood unused for three months, waiting—and the Americans argued with you and insisted that the roofs of hand-mixed concrete had to be removed because they were rotten.

Yet, in spite of the primitive conditions, the delays, the frustrations, the project moved slowly to completion within eighteen months. And the same Russian engineer permitted himself the luxury of a communistic dream:

>I am looking at the future automotive plant:
>I see the concrete road, the first in the USSR. It is smooth like the enamel of an automobile and straight like the ray of a searchlight. One hundred and forty thousand machines are moving along it, four in a row. They come from the assembly shop, the biggest shop in Europe, one and a half kilometres long. They shudder at their first touch with the hard ground on leaving the conveyor for the first time. The pressed steel building, spring shop, electric station, tool and die forge shop are planned in rows, collecting and reflecting the sun's rays in the glass of their walls. They are situated parallel to the river and behind them, among forests and parks, is the new city—it is not Novgorod; it is the City of Socialism. Like flowers in beds, there are rectangles everywhere. Every rectangle is a combination composed of a clubhouse, nursery and Kindergarten, dining hall, library, bathtubs and showers that work day and night. At the end of the city are playing fields and green parks. Its autobuses, stores, dining halls, and pavements—its gardens and its sky—are not spoiled by soot and

smoke. It is a city without chimneys and stoves, lighted by electricity and heated by steam. I cannot imagine the town otherwise than it has been drawn by the American engineers and architects.

On November 1, 1931, after eighteen months of continuous labor under the most adverse conditions, Austin successfully completed Stalin's workers' utopia and delivered its operation into the inexperienced hands of Soviet "management," management that allowed workers' committees to debate the pros and cons of a work order for hours at a time while women performed the heavy labor.

At dedication ceremonies on January 2, 1932, the massive automobile plant was given the name Molotov, in honor of the Soviet premier, and Nizhni Novgorod was renamed Gorki after the famous Russian writer. Three months later, after 90 days of operation in which exactly 2 of the anticipated 750 rear axles of the Russian-built Model A Fords had been produced, the Molotov plant was closed down. Immediately thereafter began Stalin's infamous purges, and Russia was finally dragged by the bloody scruff of its neck into the industrial twentieth century.

The Depression Deepens

By Christmas 1931, with the Russian work completed and every kopek due for the project paid and banked, the company received the devastating news that the owners of the first controlled conditions plant—after three years of research, planning, and construction—had called a halt as the project neared completion. And, as if that weren't bad enough, ex-President Calvin Coolidge had just uttered the greatest understatement of the Great Depression: "The country is not in good condition."

In 1932 Austin's and the country's business fell to its lowest ebb. The company's total contract volume had plummeted from a record high, based largely on the Autostroy project, to a low of $1,444,244—virtually all of which went out in construction wages and for materials. With its total service organization pared down to seventy-seven employees in eight districts from coast to coast, the company sent more than a hundred of its salaried personnel back into the field, and salaries of its key men, from the top down, were cut to as little as $100 a month. And these were the lucky ones. Most were simply laid off. Among the new recruits to join the growing army of the unemployed was a young engineer who had only recently joined the company. His reaction to his pink slip was as puzzling as the Depression itself: he immediately went out, put his last few dollars down on a piano, and played away his blues. Thirty years later, he became the fifth president of The Austin Company.

Prefabricated Service Stations

Despite the fact that the company's reserves were being rapidly exhausted, research activities were intensified on several fronts. They led, among other things, to the establishment, in 1933, of a new division devoted entirely to design, production, and erection of insulated steel buildings, a division that eventually became a major source of prefabricated porcelain-enamel service stations for the nation's large oil companies.

The Depression continued to drag on, and the changing of the political guard in Washington was reflected in a new adaptation of the logotype: the "pretzel" now stood side by side with the NRA eagle. But other things were changing, too—most notably the architectural form of Austin buildings.

Depression Modern: The Thirties Style

At the urging of George Bryant, The Austin Company began to look to economic recovery through the development of a distinct "modern" design that deliberately turned its back on the past and represented the future itself. This design was one born of the peculiarly American marriage of art and industry and one that displayed an impulse toward forms that were fresh and intelligent —forms that grew out of current needs, instead of archaic needs; forms that assimilated new architectural materials and functioned to meet contemporary needs. In rejecting the forms of the past and turning to starkly unadorned surfaces and glass block, stainless steel, and other modern materials, Austin thus became a pioneering exponent of the style now known as Depression Modern.[3]

Advertised in the pages of *Fortune* through the use of strik-

[3] George A. Bryant—who had joined the organization in 1913 in Canada as a field engineer and clerk, and whom *Business Week* was later to call "a man who eats, sleeps, and thinks Austin"—was appointed general manager of the company in 1930. The ideas generated in response to his challenge to find ways to design and build economical plants of greater utility, more flexibility, and better appearance produced some of the best examples of the Depression Modern style in America. Many of these buildings were designed by Austin architect Robert Smith, Jr.

ingly original models, the style gradually began to catch on and to suggest the industrial landscape of the future. Ideally, the Depression Modern style was spare. Although the earliest examples did exhibit a certain amount of decorative detail, the style became purer and purer, until, finally, an Austin building in the Depression Modern vogue could be said to be without a single detail that could be called extraneous, without any embellishment, without a line that did not seem inevitable. There was nothing in Depression Modern to distract the eye or mind. It was clean and uncluttered, direct and innocently American. Austin's contributions to the style—most notably the NBC Radio City of the West and the Church and Dwight plant, two masterpieces of the '30s—will be generously sampled in the gallery that follows.

Austin's work in the final years of the Depression was not influenced by the European modernism—labeled by designer Russel Wright as "packing-crate modernism"—that began to influence American architecture after the Museum of Modern Art's Bauhaus exhibition in 1938. Its Depression Modern style, consequently, was very American in scale, strength, and self-confidence, prompting a critic in the *AIA Journal* to "wonder what America might have been able to develop if it had not again suffered one of its many European invasions, namely that of the Bauhaus designers in the late '30s and early '40s."

The first *Fortune* advertisement employing a prototype model, May 1935.

Survival

By 1937, as a result of its pathbreaking advertising campaign in *Fortune*, Austin suddenly found itself with more business than it ever had before—the bulk of it in striking projects that attracted national and international attention. And in 1938, just as fluorescent lighting had been perfected, the company for which Austin had built the first controlled conditions plant requested that it be put in operation. When the Simonds Saw and Steel factory opened later that year, it was the most modern in the world—inside. Outside it wore the Art Deco façade designed for it in 1929. Ironically, no factor in the years since 1929 had done more to render Art Deco obsolete than Austin itself.

In the final days of summer 1939, a resurgent economy permitted The Austin Company to announce the forthcoming expansion of its Cleveland engineering facilities in a new building that would serve as a showplace for its newly-developed rigid frame design. In a sense, the new building was to be a symbolic phoenix emerging from the ashes of the Great Depression. Samuel Austin would have been pleased, although hardly surprised, at his company's determined survival. But a few weeks before his eighty-sixth birthday, three years before, he had died on May 23, 1936.

As news of the new engineering building was released, George Bryant was aboard the last train from Berlin to Moscow on his way to inspect the workers' city that Austin had built at the beginning of the decade. He had just passed through the Polish corridor as Nazi and Soviet forces, in an instant of premeditated madness, plunged the world into the nightmare of World War II.

THE AUSTIN COMPANY
ENGINEERS
CLEVELAND, OHIO, U.S.A.
AUTOMOBILE PLANT PROJECT
for
AUTOSTROY
NIJNI NOVGOROD, U.S.S.R.
GENERAL PLAN
WORKER'S CITY AND PLANT
SCALE 1:20,000

WORKER'S CITY
Index

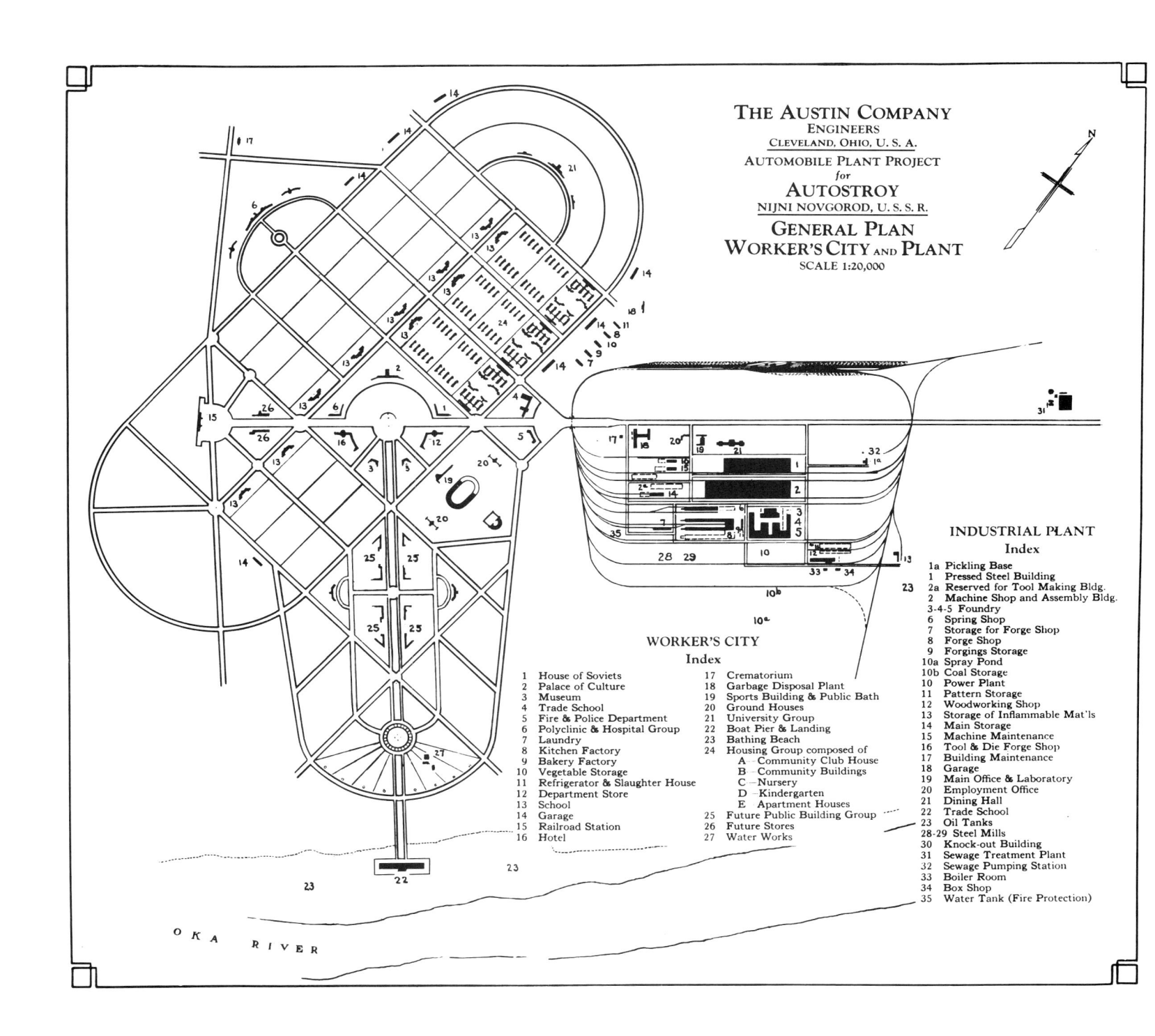

1. House of Soviets
2. Palace of Culture
3. Museum
4. Trade School
5. Fire & Police Department
6. Polyclinic & Hospital Group
7. Laundry
8. Kitchen Factory
9. Bakery Factory
10. Vegetable Storage
11. Refrigerator & Slaughter House
12. Department Store
13. School
14. Garage
15. Railroad Station
16. Hotel
17. Crematorium
18. Garbage Disposal Plant
19. Sports Building & Public Bath
20. Ground Houses
21. University Group
22. Boat Pier & Landing
23. Bathing Beach
24. Housing Group composed of
    - A — Community Club House
    - B — Community Buildings
    - C — Nursery
    - D — Kindergarten
    - E — Apartment Houses
25. Future Public Building Group
26. Future Stores
27. Water Works

INDUSTRIAL PLANT
Index

1a. Pickling Base
1. Pressed Steel Building
2a. Reserved for Tool Making Bldg.
2. Machine Shop and Assembly Bldg.
3-4-5. Foundry
6. Spring Shop
7. Storage for Forge Shop
8. Forge Shop
9. Forgings Storage
10a. Spray Pond
10b. Coal Storage
10. Power Plant
11. Pattern Storage
12. Woodworking Shop
13. Storage of Inflammable Mat'ls
14. Main Storage
15. Machine Maintenance
16. Tool & Die Forge Shop
17. Building Maintenance
18. Garage
19. Main Office & Laboratory
20. Employment Office
21. Dining Hall
22. Trade School
23. Oil Tanks
28-29. Steel Mills
30. Knock-out Building
31. Sewage Treatment Plant
32. Sewage Pumping Station
33. Boiler Room
34. Box Shop
35. Water Tank (Fire Protection)

OKA RIVER

The great size of the workers' city and automobile plant designed for the USSR in 1929–30 and completed in 1931 may be seen from the general plan, *above*, drawn on a scale of 1:20,000. The original plan called for more than 150 different buildings. *Opposite:* Aerial view of complete automobile plant (1931); George A. Bryant signing the Autostroy contract (1929).

АВТОЗАВОД
Н-НОВГОРОД
СССР

108

Opposite: Special engineering department set up in rented offices in Cleveland to design Russian project; peasant women employed as construction workers (1930). *Left:* Portions of the project under construction (1930); aerial view of workers' city (1931).

109

For a brief period Austin styled its structures in the modernistic (Art Deco) mode. *Right:* Cleveland Airport (1929); storefront, Seattle, Washington (1929). *Below:* Lobby, Carnegie Medical Building, Cleveland, Ohio (1929). *Opposite:* People's Mutual Building, Beverly Hills, California (1931); Goodyear Pavillion, Chicago Century of Progress Exposition (1933).

111

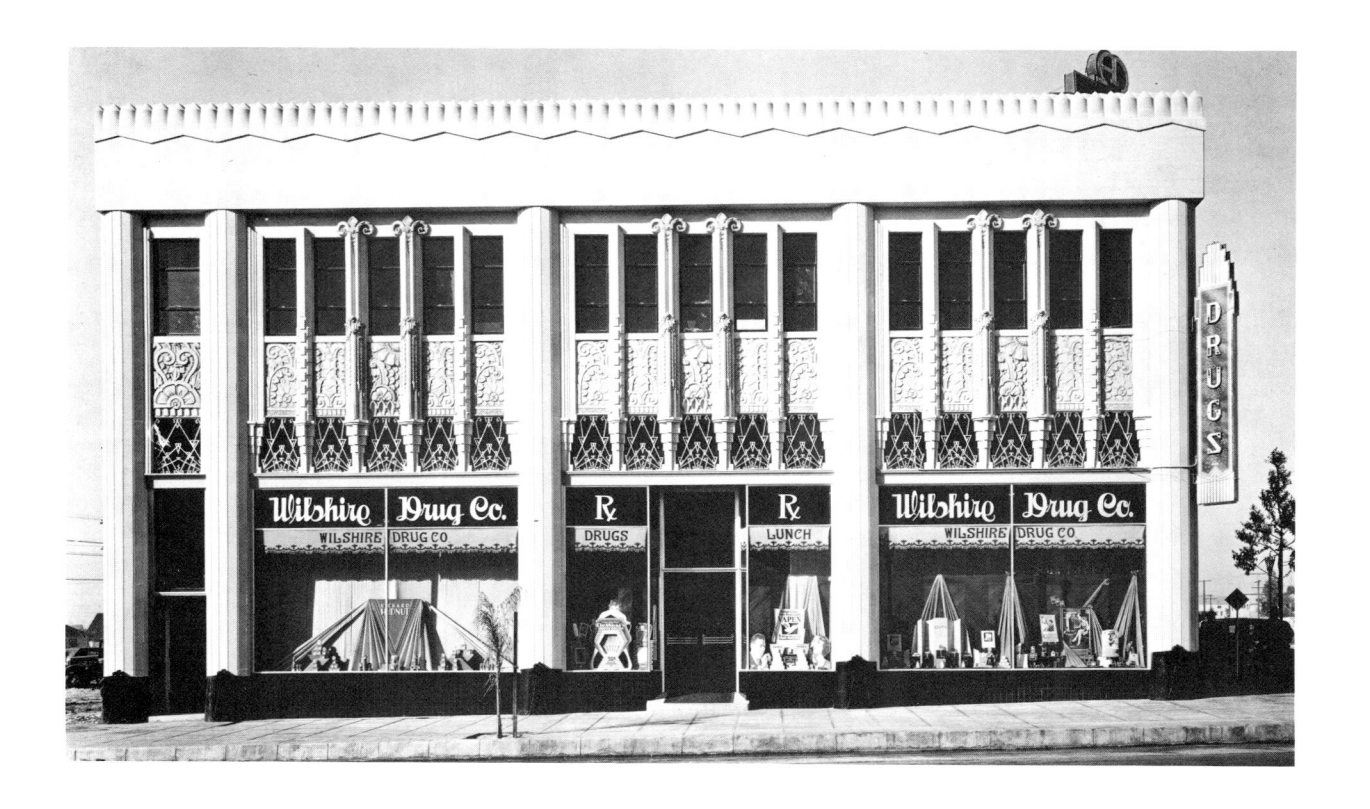

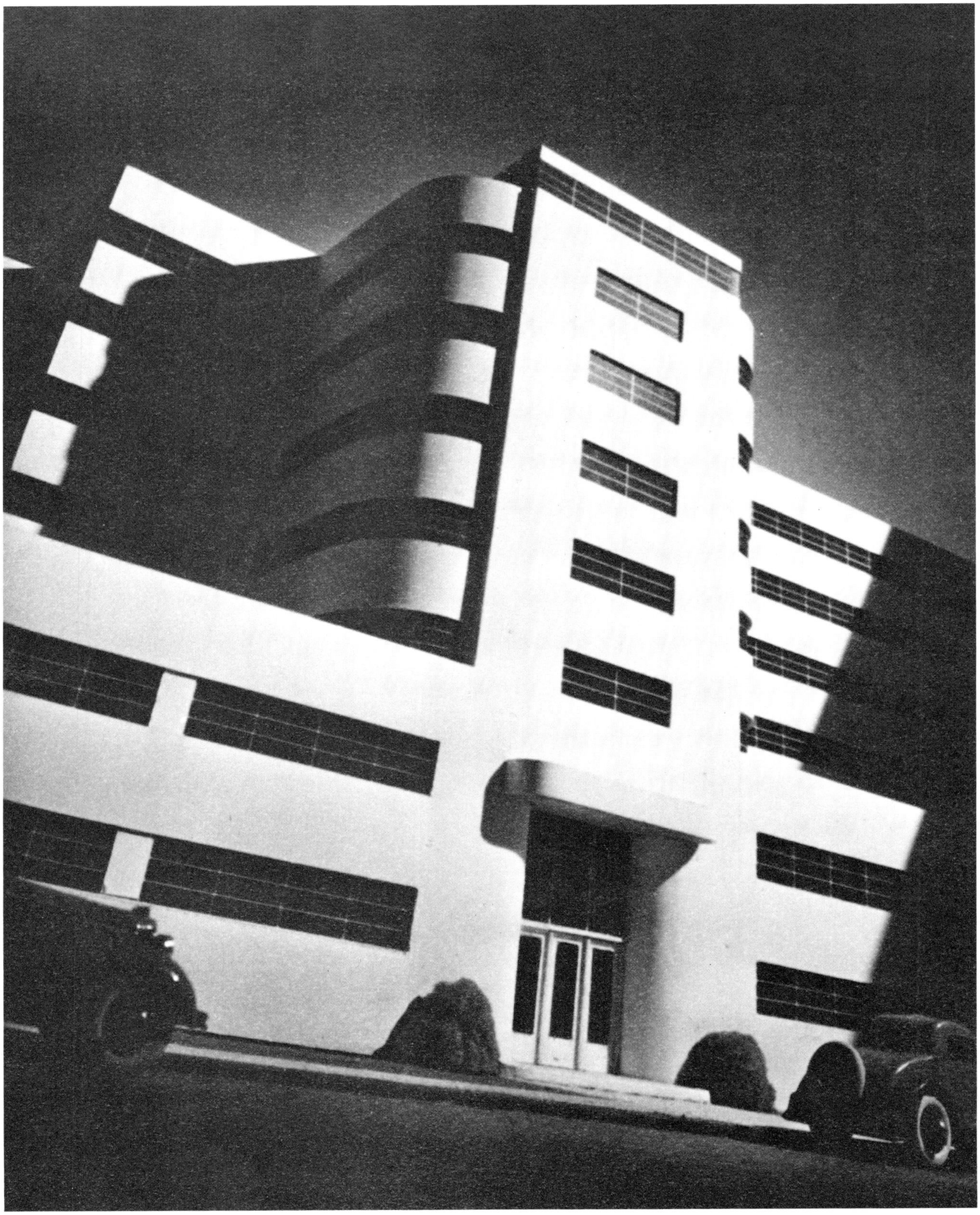

In 1935, Austin launched an advertising campaign in *Fortune* magazine employing prototype models of advanced Depression Modern design which stimulated thinking about the plants of the future. These models helped to establish new goals and standards for design and construction and emphasized the economic benefits of architectural functionalism.

114

Austin's prototype models underlined the importance of the modern-designed plant as a means of meeting competition in times of economic duress. Although the models were originally "dream-concepts" designed in the midst of the Great Depression, when Austin's business was at its lowest ebb, the prototypes led directly to several important design and construction contracts in the late '30s. NBC's Radio City of the West (1938) and the Church and Dwight plant (1939) conform almost exactly to their prototype models.

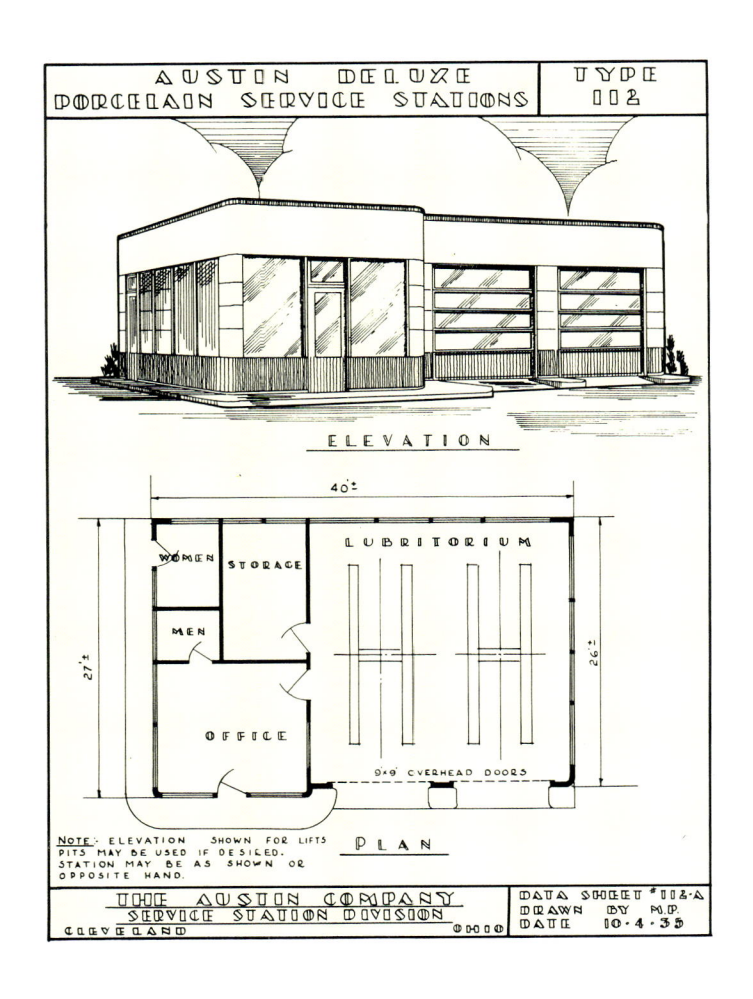

Few designs of the Depression had a greater impact on the American landscape than Austin's prefabricated porcelain-enamel service stations. *Left:* Data sheet (1935). *Above:* Cleveland, Ohio (1937). *Below:* Little Rock, Arkansas (1939). *Opposite:* Cincinnati, Ohio (1934); Cleveland, Ohio (1936).

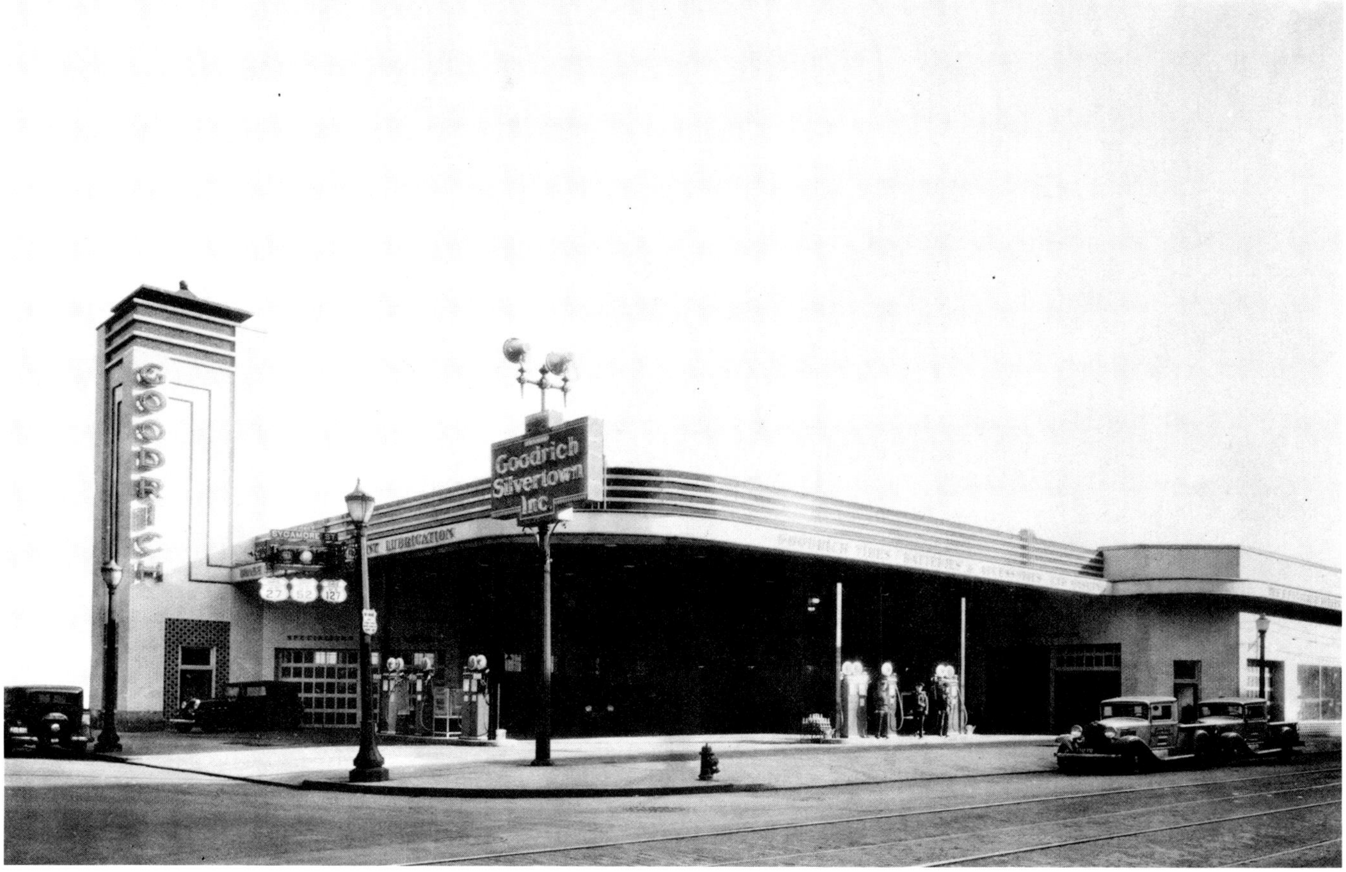
Goodrich
Silvertown
Inc.
LUBRICATION

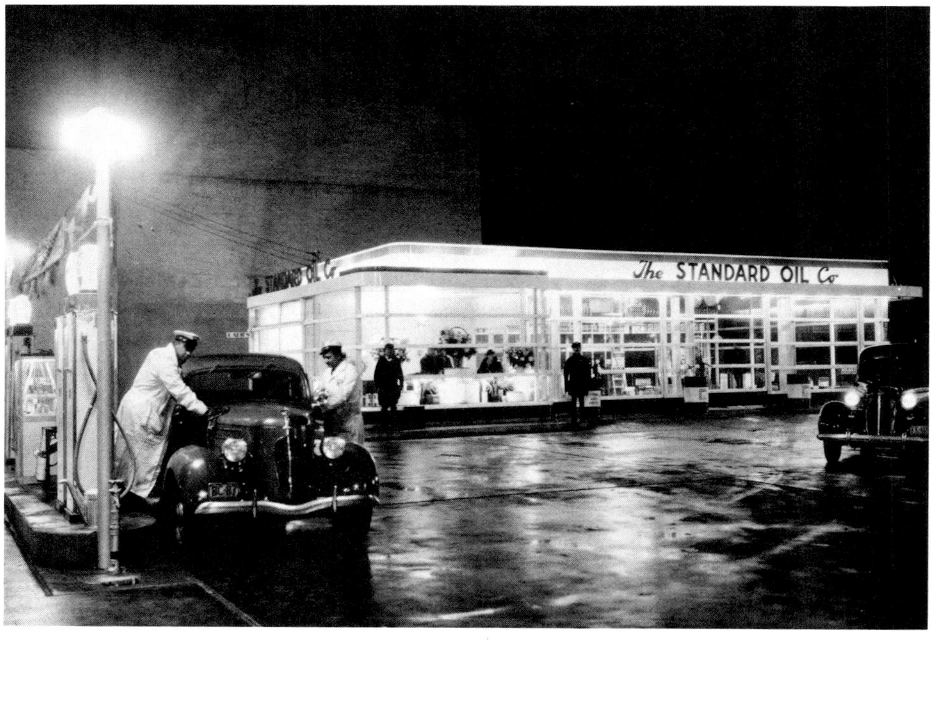
The STANDARD OIL Co

NINETEEN-THIRTY
modernization year in industry

Mighty buildings rear their heads into the clouds . . . sturdy ships of the air drone away to distant ports . . . new products appear overnight on counters and in salesrooms everywhere.

It is a dramatic age in which industry plays a lead role, for back of all the romantic pageant are the wheels that must turn, ever faster, to set the pace of progress.

And so, *1930—Modernization Year in Industry*, marks a New Era in the design and construction of the Nation's plants . . . an Era in which Austin will be called upon to accomplish still greater achievements in producing plants to supply modern demands.

Austin's nation-wide organization is busy from Coast to Coast . . . designing and building a number of modern plants that herald the New Era in American Industry.

Executives in practically every field of business will find Austin literature, which deals with fundamentals as well as specific building problems, helpful. Wire, phone or write the nearest Austin office for the literature and approximate costs on any project you may be planning.

THE AUSTIN COMPANY
ENGINEERS AND BUILDERS · · · CLEVELAND

THE AUSTIN METHOD OF UNDIVIDED RESPONSIBILITY
Design, construction and building equipment . . . . separate responsibilities ordinarily . . . . become one unified responsibility under The Austin Method. One organization handles the complete project under one contract which guarantees in advance, total cost, time of completion with bonus and penalty clause if desired; and quality of materials and workmanship.

New York   Chicago   Philadelphia   Newark   Detroit   Cincinnati
Pittsburgh   St. Louis   Seattle   Portland   Phoenix
The Austin Company of California Ltd.: Los Angeles, Oakland and San Francisco
The Austin Company of Texas: Dallas   The Austin Company of Canada, Limited

This Austin advertisement appears in the March issue of Fortune.

Whether employing the modernistic drawings of the early '30s or the Depression Modern prototype models in the years after 1935, Austin's advertisements of the Depression were in the vanguard of American graphic design. *Opposite: Fortune* (March, 1930). *Left* (*above*): *Fortune* (August, 1930). *Left* (*below*): *Nation's Business* (July, 1929). *Below: Fortune* (April, 1936).

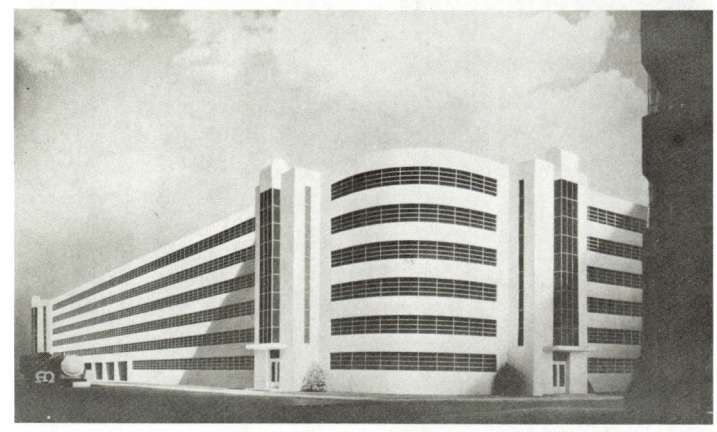

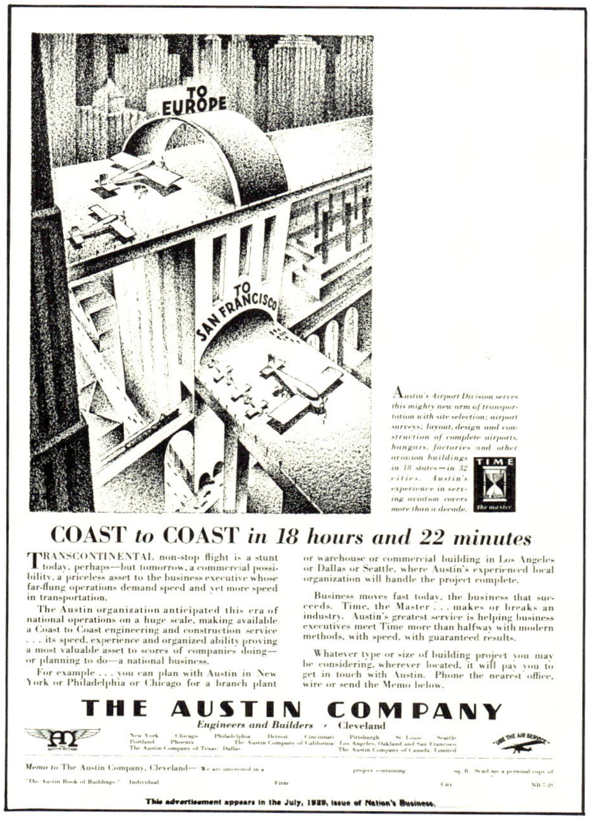

A few of the outstanding Austin structures of the Depression: *Right:* Wilbert J. Austin Engineering Building, Cleveland, Ohio (1939–40). *Below (left)*: NBC Studios, Hollywood, California (1935). Radio was the one industry whose growth was *aided* by the Depression. These studios, consequently, were outgrown by the time the building opened, necessitating the construction of Hollywood's new Radio City in 1938. *Below (right)*: Hills Bros. Coffee, Inc., Edgewater, New Jersey (1939). *Opposite:* Research Laboratory, American Rolling Mills, Middletown, Ohio (1936); Plant and General Offices, All-Steel-Equip Company, Aurora, Illinois (1940).

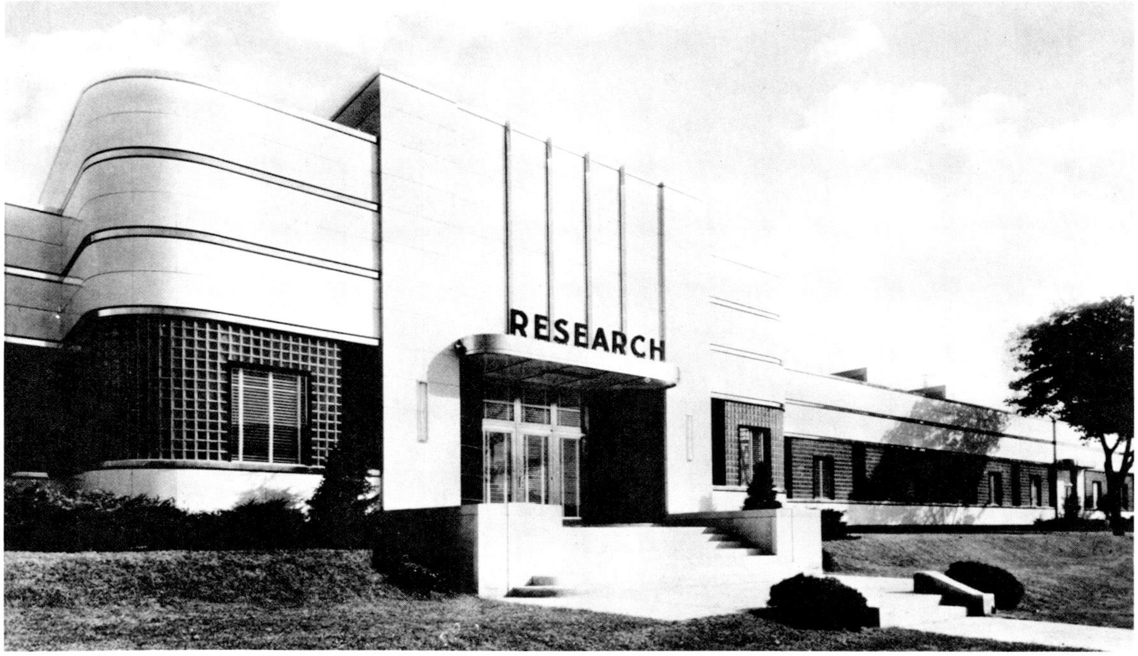
RESEARCH

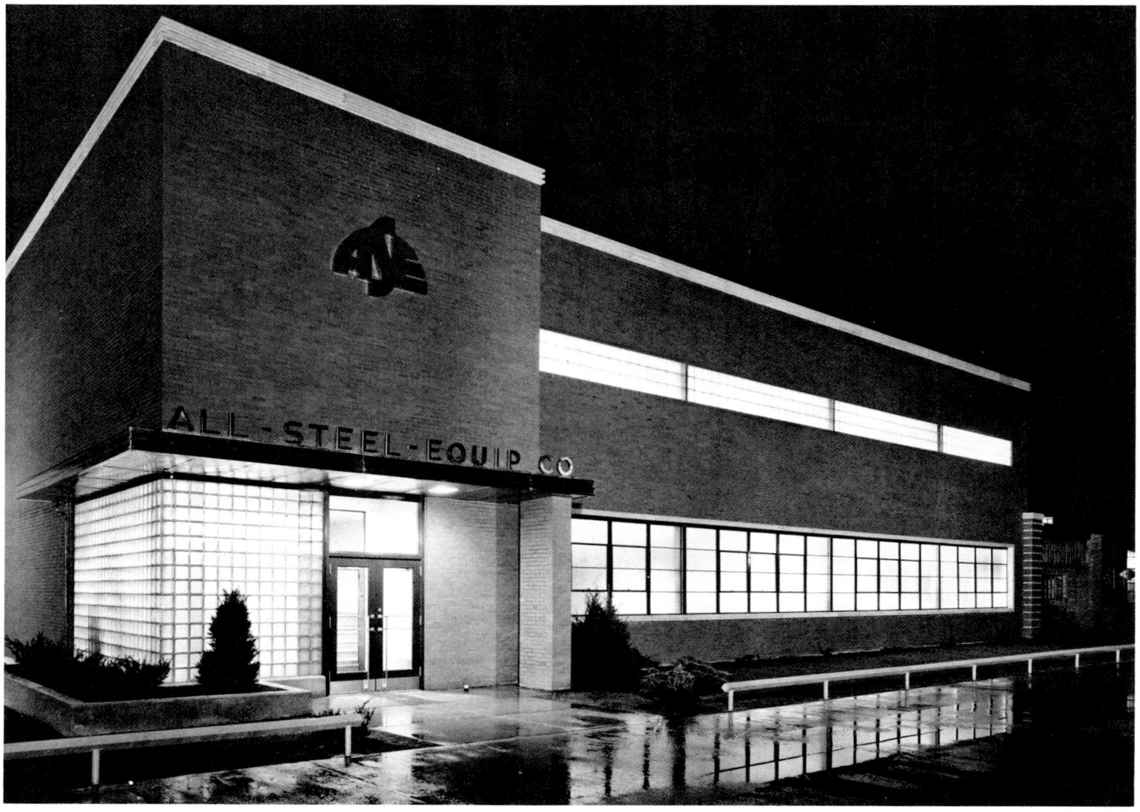
ALL-STEEL-EQUIP CO

PROPOSED · ASSEMBLY · BUILDING
· BOEING · AIRCRAFT · COMPANY ·

Other projects of the late '30s included several for the Boeing Aircraft Company, Seattle, Washington, among which was the assembly building (1936), pictured *above*. *Right:* Austin's success in building porcelain-enamel service stations led to the development of drive-in laundries and the nation's first prefabricated porcelain-enamel supermarkets. Pictured here is an Acme market in Akron, Ohio (1939). *Opposite:* Antrol Laboratories, Inc., Los Angeles, California (1937). In 1937 Austin pioneered by designing and constructing a prestressed concrete water storage tank with a 1.5 million gallon capacity for Crown Zellerbach Corporation, Camas, Washington.

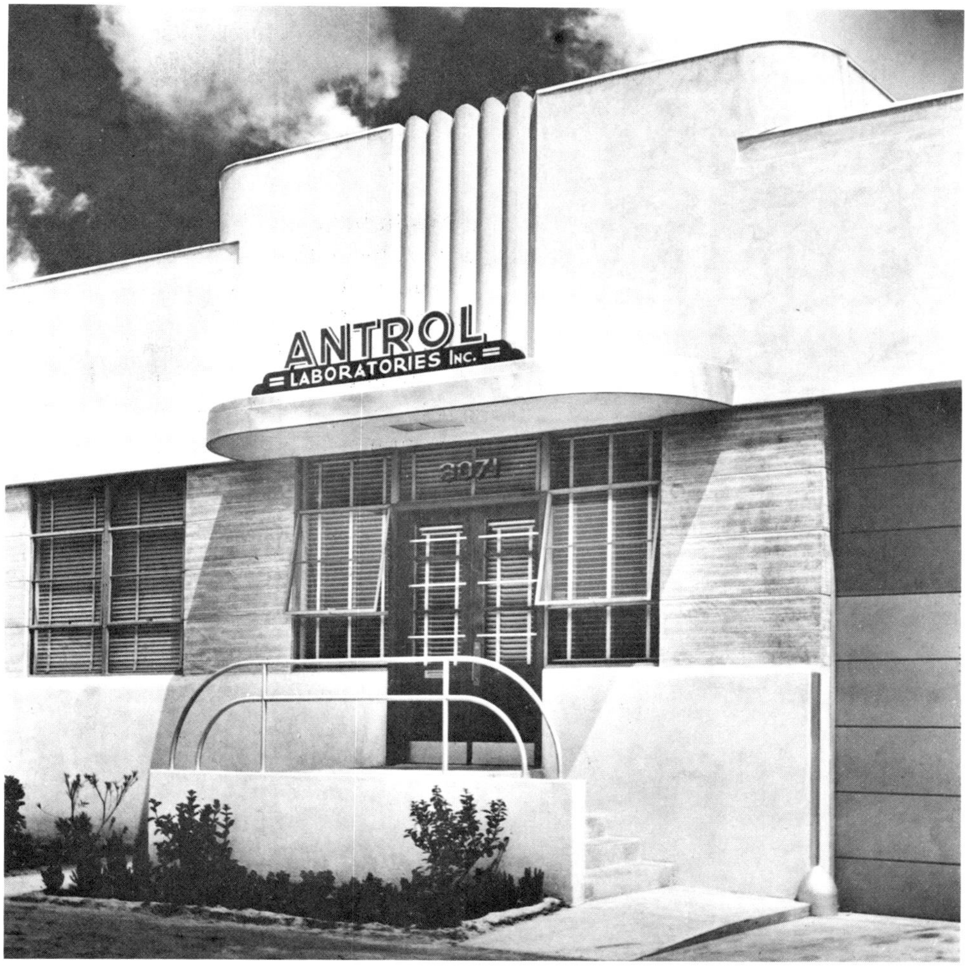
ANTROL
LABORATORIES INC.

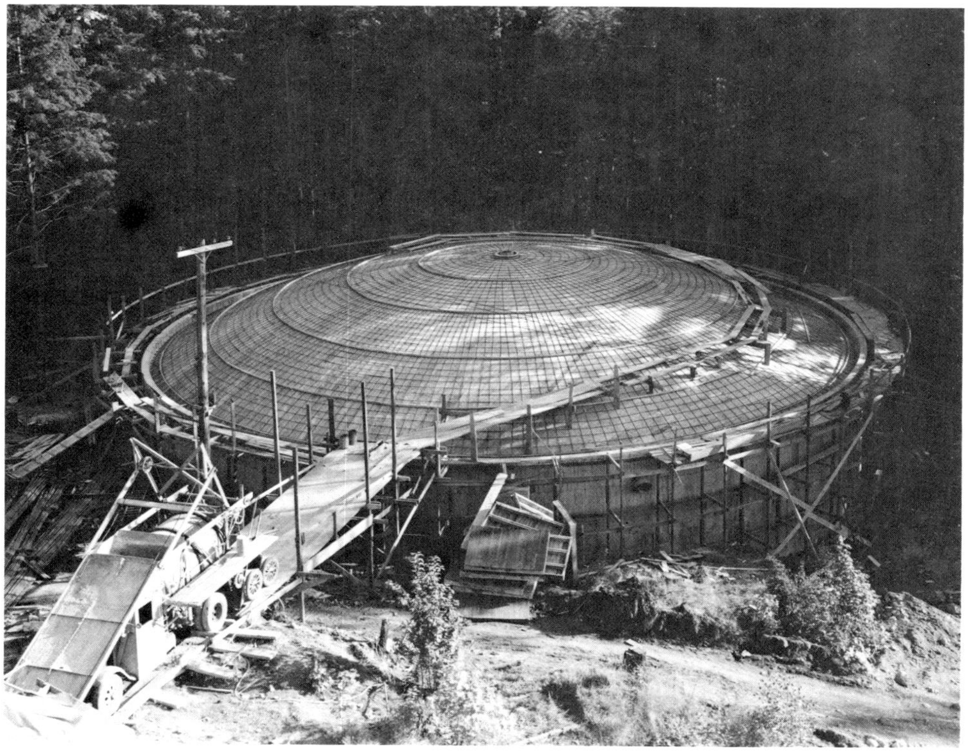

Two Austin buildings, typical of the Depression Modern style: horizontal bias, bold curves, lavish employment of glass block and other "modern" materials (stainless steel, porcelain enamel, etc.). Note, at *left*, the three horizontal bands, ubiquitous in Depression design and suggestive of streamlining—dubbed by one architectural critic as "the unholy trinity" of 1930s industrial design. *Left:* Precision Spring Corp., Detroit, Michigan (1936). *Below:* Phoenix Laboratory, General Motors Sales Corp., Phoenix, Arizona (1937).

One of two unqualified Austin landmarks of Depression design—the Church and Dwight plant, Syracuse, New York (1939). The makers of Arm & Hammer Baking Soda required a structure reflecting the purity of their product, and Austin, consequently, designed a white brick, air-conditioned building in which the only ornamentation was its pattern of fenestration, a pattern dictated largely by function. The basic curve of the plant, that which gives it its singular shape, is purely functional: it is built around a seven-story industrial tank, necessary for the production of the company's product. The building suggests why Walter Dorwin Teague, impressed by the simple lines of late '30s design, wrote that "Americans achieve a high degree of simplicity because they are primitives in this new machine age."

In a race to equate network prestige with architectural excellence, CBS engaged William Lescaze to design its Hollywood studios while, only one block away, NBC relied upon the Austin Method. Austin's Radio City of the West (1938) was, in a word, one of the few American architectural masterpieces of the Depression.

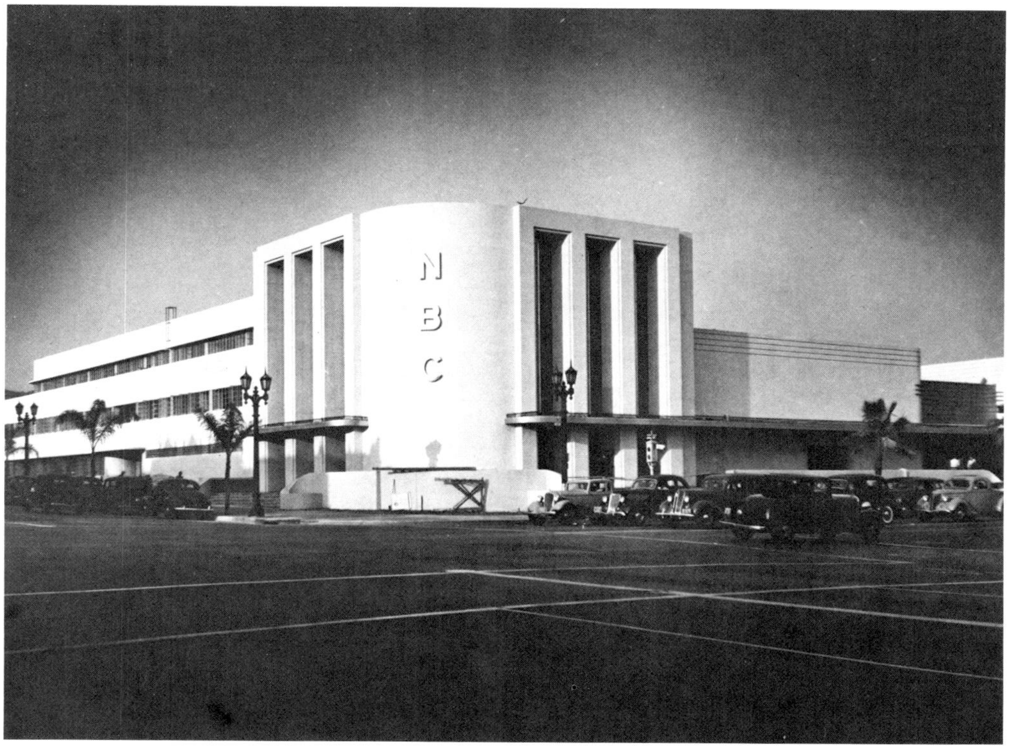
N
B
C

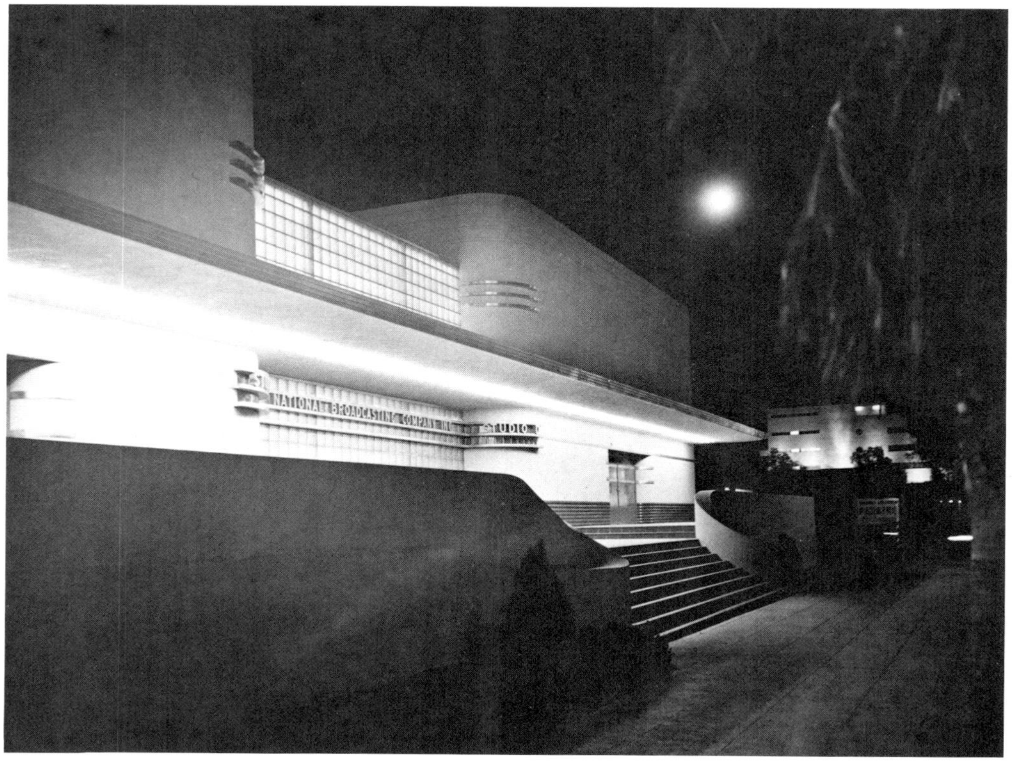
NATIONAL BROADCASTING COMPANY INC
STUDIO

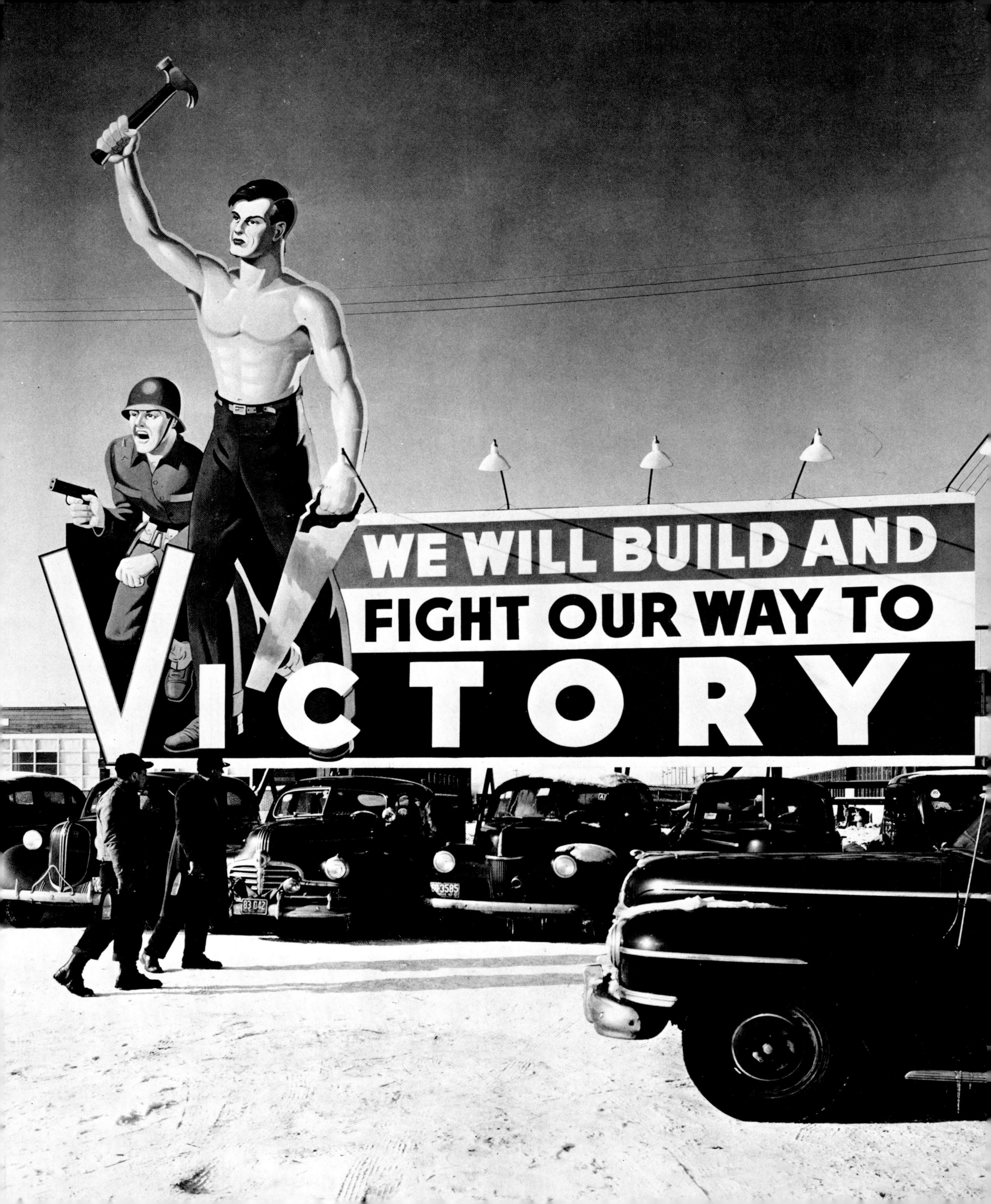
WE WILL BUILD AND
FIGHT OUR WAY TO
VICTORY

IV Austin Goes to War

The "Blackout" Plant

Austin went to war—unwittingly—the very day the first controlled conditions plant had been developed. The original conception of this revolutionary plant, inside of which "the conditions prevailing out-of-doors on a perfect June afternoon would be reproduced 24 hours a day the year 'round," had been born of conversations between J. K. Gannett, Austin's eastern district manager, and Gifford K. Simonds, then manager of the Simonds Saw and Steel Company, for whom Austin belatedly completed the first such plant in 1938.

Now, under the impetus of wartime needs which emphasized the value of blackout protection provided by such windowless factories, hundreds of American industries from coast to coast began to apply the principles of complete light, sound, and atmospheric control which were first proven by the successful operation of the Simonds plant.

When the outbreak of hostilities in Europe in 1939 forced large-scale expansion of America's aviation industries, The Austin Company turned its knowledge of controlled conditions and high-speed construction techniques to good account.

The world's second windowless factory was designed and built by Austin in 1939 for the division of the General Motors Corporation which manufactured Allison liquid-cooled aircraft engines, a product that would be in widespread use throughout the war in Army fighting planes and pursuit ships. Begun in June, a few months before the outbreak of war, this vital defense plant had not been designed specifically for blackout protection, but rather to insure the controlled conditions necessary to obtain the precision required in such high-powered units. The General Motors management realized that the surest way to eliminate rejections and scrap was to control light and humidity, either of which might be the cause of many difficulties. If, for instance, an engine casting stood awhile in the sunlight and was machined before all radiant heat had disappeared, it would never conform to the fine tolerance specified for most Allison parts. Similarly, rust started by a sweaty palm would be just about as harmful to finished engine parts.

All of these hazards were adequately met in a well insulated masonry structure, equipped with the latest fluorescent lighting and a number of medium-sized air-conditioning units, which were

Opposite: Victory sign at the construction site of Chicago's Douglas Aircraft Assembly Plant, 1943.

located in penthouses at strategic points above the working area. This basic design was followed, practically without change, in extensions which more than trebled the size of Allison's original controlled conditions plant during the war. More importantly, it also set the pattern for the great majority of blackout plants erected in the war years.

The following year, 1940, the Grumman Aircraft Engineering Corporation required a new engineering building at Bethpage, Long Island, and Austin designed a controlled conditions structure for this purpose. The ideal working conditions enjoyed there by the Grumman staff led to the choice of an Austin windowless design when an influx of war orders for Grumman fighter and torpedo planes forced a large expansion of the company's facilities.

During the next five years, and at a cost of more than 100 million dollars, Austin built 11 blackout plants designed for the production and equipping of military aircraft under controlled conditions, while another 100 million dollars worth of more conventional structures for aircraft production were being completed by its engineering staff.

W. J. Austin and Aviation

Thus the company that had built the world's largest aircraft plant only twenty-two years earlier in World War I and had gone on to pioneer in the design of modern hangers, wind tunnels, dirigible mooring masts, and complete airports in the '20s and '30s, now found itself thrust by the exigencies of a war economy into the position of being the nation's largest builder of military aircraft plants.

The man most directly responsible for The Austin Company's primacy in aviation construction was Wilbert J. Austin, one of the nation's earliest advocates and patrons of air travel. He had flown more than a half-million miles in commercial transport planes and felt personally closer to aviation than to any other industry. His interest was reflected in the many aircraft projects designed and built by the company during his lifetime, and he himself was a director of two air transport firms. It was a tragic irony, then, that attended his death in the crash of a commercial airliner in Chicago during a blinding snowstorm on December 4, 1940, only a few short months after he had been awarded the honorary degree of doctor of engineering by the Case Institute of Technology. At the time of his death, he had been actively devoting his energies to getting his company into high gear for the national defence emergency. Sadly, but appropriately, The Austin Company's new engineering buiding was dedicated in his memory five months later.

War Projects The Austin Company's war work included numerous ship building facilities, machine tool factories, two major penicillin plants, an air base in Alaska, several factories for the manufacture of electronic instruments and devices, the conversion of space in a metropolitan office building for the controlled conditions manufacture of bombsights as well as the design and construction of a new controlled conditions plant for producing the strategically important Norden bombsight, the design of special Naval facilities, and America's largest wind tunnel—an aeronautical "test-tube" designed for the Boeing Company and capable of generating super-hurricanes approaching the speed of sound.

The Major Bomber Assembly Plants The highlight of the war years, however, was the design and construction of three mammoth controlled conditions Army aircraft plants in the Southwest, for which the company developed "breathing" walls as an aid to economical air-conditioning. The most spectacular of these were the twin bomber assembly plants at Forth Worth (Consolidated-Vultee) and at Tulsa (Douglas) where the lightweight insulated fiberglas and steel panel walls paved the way for the development of modern curtain-wall techniques. White fiberglas that combined light-reflecting and acoustical properties lined the interiors, and each had a floor of white cement which insured maximum upward reflection of the light that originated in the rectified fluorescent fixtures along its high 4,000-foot long assembly bay. Austin's eventual expansion of the Fort Worth plant (1942) into a completely integrated aircraft plant made it the world's second largest air-conditioned building, second only to the Pentagon.

Following government metal-conservation directives which made impossible the use of steel walls in the third major bomber plant project (Douglas Aircraft, Oklahoma City, 1943), Austin developed a "breathing" masonry wall which employed some 17.5 million bricks to duplicate the effectiveness of the insulation in the other plants. The same need to conserve steel led to the construction of an enormous all-timber Army aircraft plant at Chicago in the same year. (Austin had, of course, been required to build all-timber structures during World War I, and in the 1920s had also built the first Hollywood sound stages of wood.)

Austin's Army-Navy "E"

One far-reaching contract led directly to a particularly proud event in Austin's war on the home front. Early in 1943, 4,600 West Coast engineers and construction workers associated with the company on Navy engineering and construction work aggregating 70 million dollars received the Army-Navy "E" award, the first such award for construction in the Pacific Northwest. The projects under this contract included four air stations, two air domes, two radio stations, a fuel depot, a supply depot, an ammunition depot, a hospital, a number of complete section bases, air fields, and schools—plus a number of other structures for the Army and the Coast Guard. The company had been commended for furnishing "all that it takes to make a complete job—engineering, management, construction." "Your company," the citation read, "has always enjoyed a reputation for fast construction. Under this Navy contract that reputation has been even more firmly established." Wilbert Austin, who had originally made possible the company's reputation for speed, would have been pleased. George Bryant, the new president of The Austin Company, accepted the award with gratitude.

In the course of its work on these Northwest projects, Austin built the first prestressed concrete tanks ever used for fuel storage and developed a new type of construction for seaplane ramps which used beams and slabs of precast concrete. This eliminated the need for cofferdam construction, which would have been costly and would have required a great amount of steel. The saving of steel in the original design was later extended by the substitution of laminated wood reinforcing for steel in the slabs.

Special Devices Division

When the Navy's Bureau of Aeronautics turned to industry in 1943 for aid in the development of synthetic combat training devices, Austin staffed a new division with a special group of electrical and mechanical engineers. The success of this Special Devices Division in the development, manufacture, and installation of training devices to increase the effectiveness of torpedo planes and submarine crews in combat led to the retention of the division in peacetime and its gradual evolution into today's Austin Advanced Technology Systems.

Planning for Peace

As it passed its peak of wartime activity in the same year, Austin shifted its emphasis to research and to preparing its men for the stiff business competition that would surely come with peace. There had been a reservoir of capital and technology amassed during the war that would bring many new companies and new products into the industrial spectrum. Austin wanted to be ready for these changes. And it was.

One area in which it concentrated assured it a leading place in the postwar sun. And that area was television. The Austin Company was convinced that the end of war would bring the American consumer increased leisure time and that television, consequently, was going to be a major growth industry of the postwar era, a notion ridiculed by many businessmen, including Time Inc's Henry Luce who believed that no medium could ever displace the primacy of radio. Nonetheless, Austin developed a television studio construction program two years before the end of the war, resolute in its belief that returning G. I. Joes would be all too happy to spend the coming years in an easy chair before a flickering tube. It could not have been more correct—or financially astute.

But by the time Joe came home, went through his G. I. bill schooling, waited for industry to retool and for the housing shortage to ease, and finally could afford a television set, he had to move his wife and kids and the TV set out to the suburbs—where the jobs had moved.

And Austin moved with him.

Unveiling the working model of a large television network studio, April 1944.

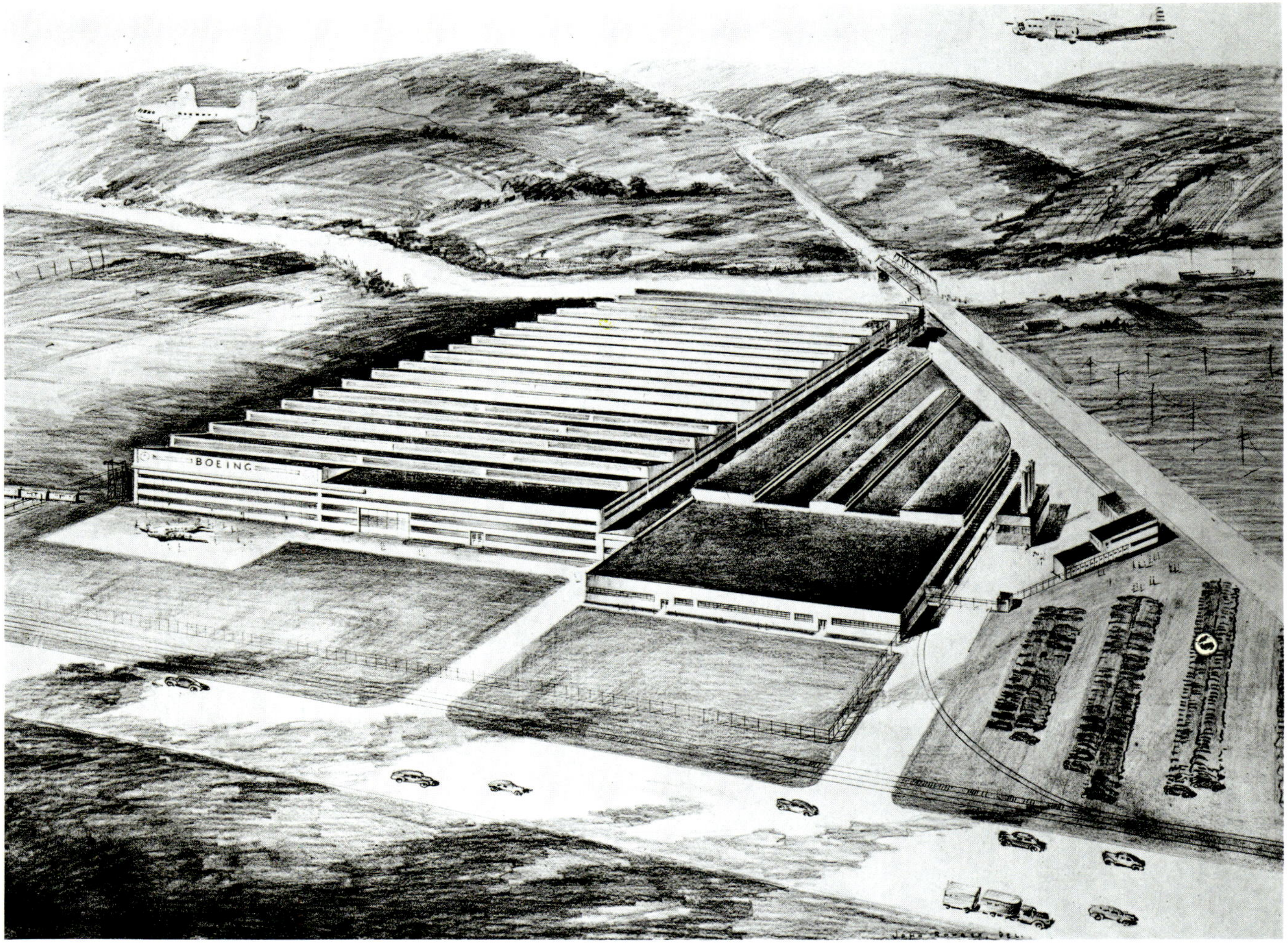
BOEING

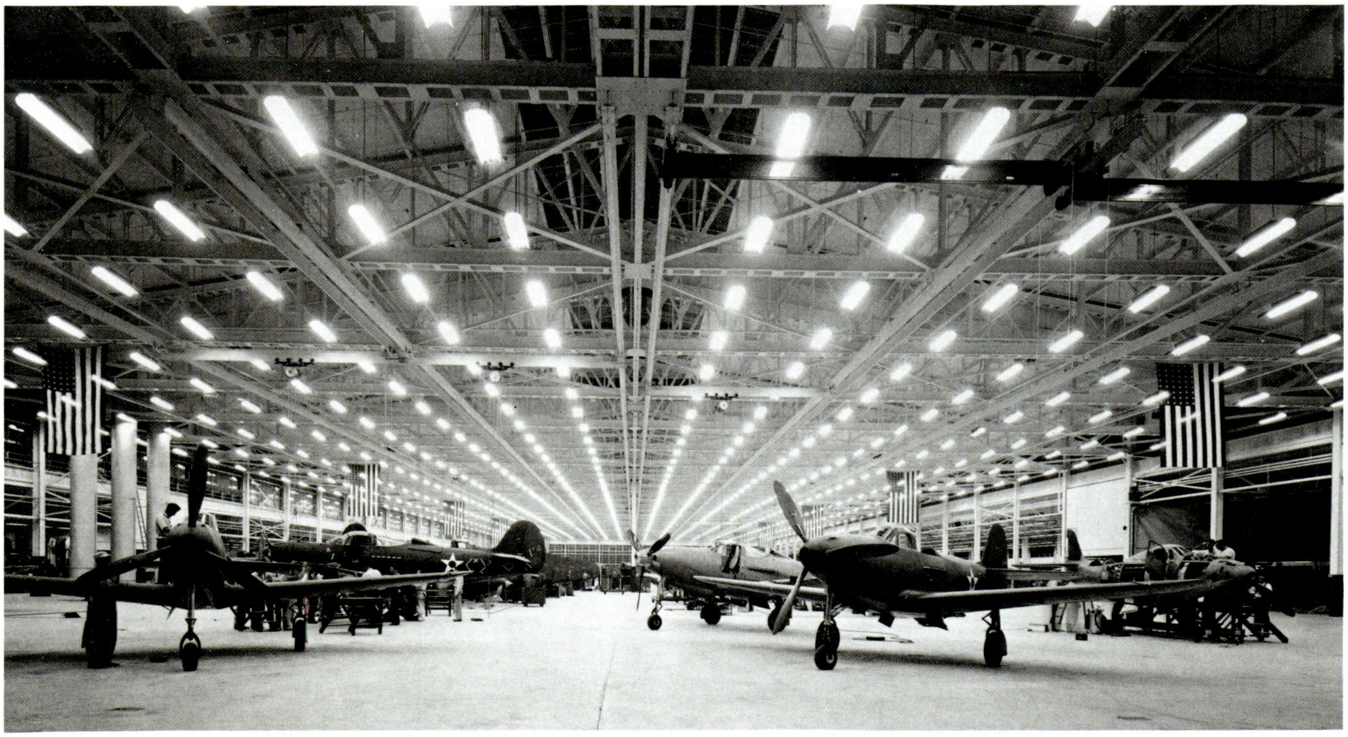

War defense work before and after Pearl Harbor. *Opposite:* Boeing Aircraft Company Plant No. 2, Seattle, Washington (1940); Assembly plant, Bell Aircraft Corporation, Niagara Falls, New York (1941). *Above:* Boeing wind tunnel (1944).

Three views of the Douglas Aircraft "Blackout" Plant, Oklahoma City, Oklahoma (1942–43). Austin engineers eliminated 200 tons of critical materials by the use of non-metallic reflectors in the fluorescent lighting mechanism, *above*. (The reflectors were masonite with a synthetic white enamel surface and illuminated the working area which had a floor of reflective white cement.) This plant, which was the world's largest masonry structure, contained 17 million bricks in its "breathing" walls. Douglas C-47 Skytrains, *opposite*, are seen by the mammoth hangar, which featured three telescoping turn-over doors on either side.

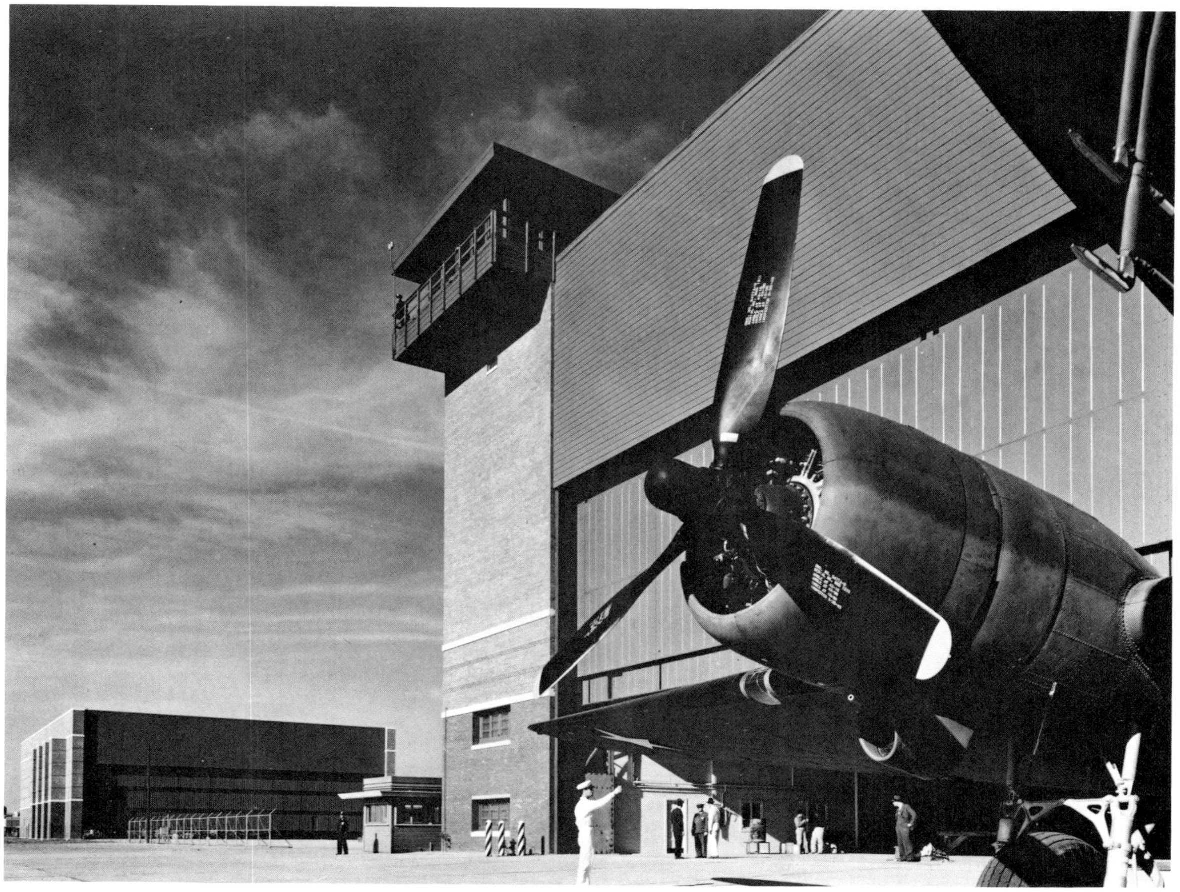

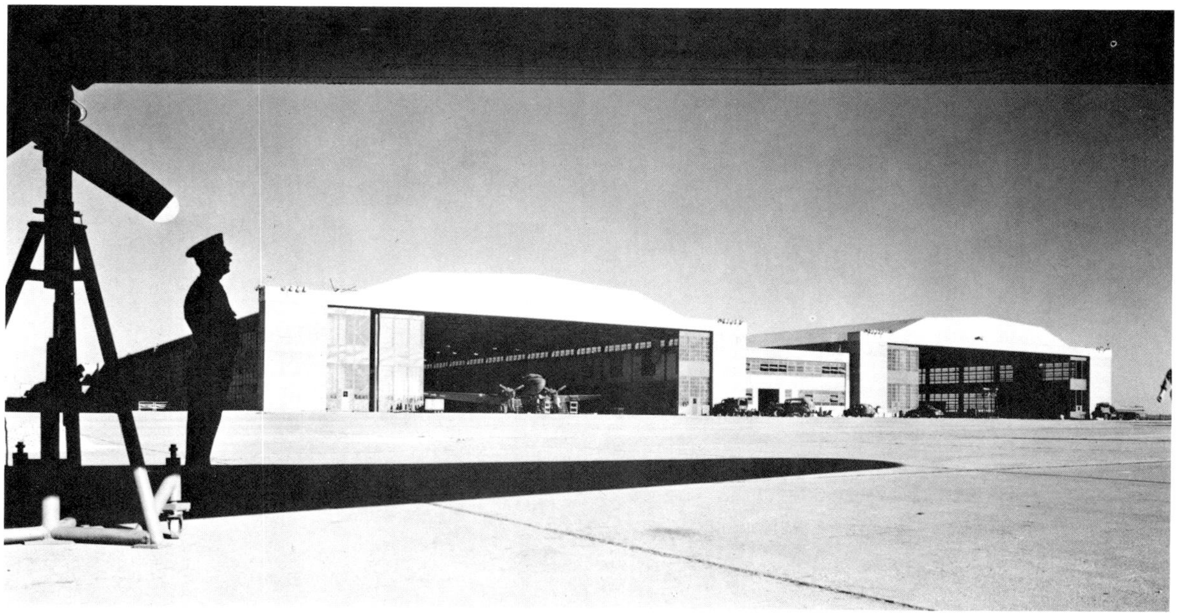

Steel and Fiberglas "breathing" walls made Consolidated-Vultee's Fort Worth, Texas, plant (1942) the world's outstanding example of controlled-conditions design. It was the first to combine rectified fluorescent lighting, light-reflecting Fiberglas walls and ceiling, and a white cement floor, in a floor-to-ceiling approach to illumination problems, *below. Opposite:* The air-conditioned hangar had four 200-foot spans and a working space 200 by 400 feet on either side of a brick fire wall in the center. The construction view shows less than half of the huge assembly building.

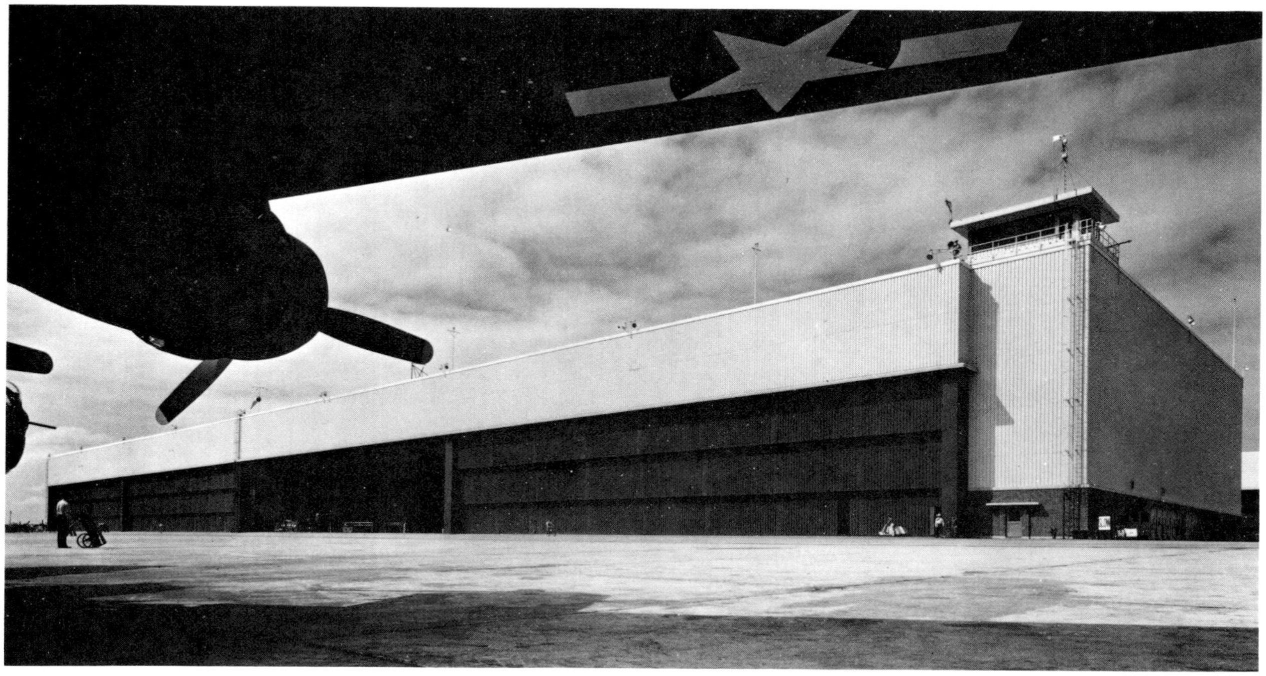

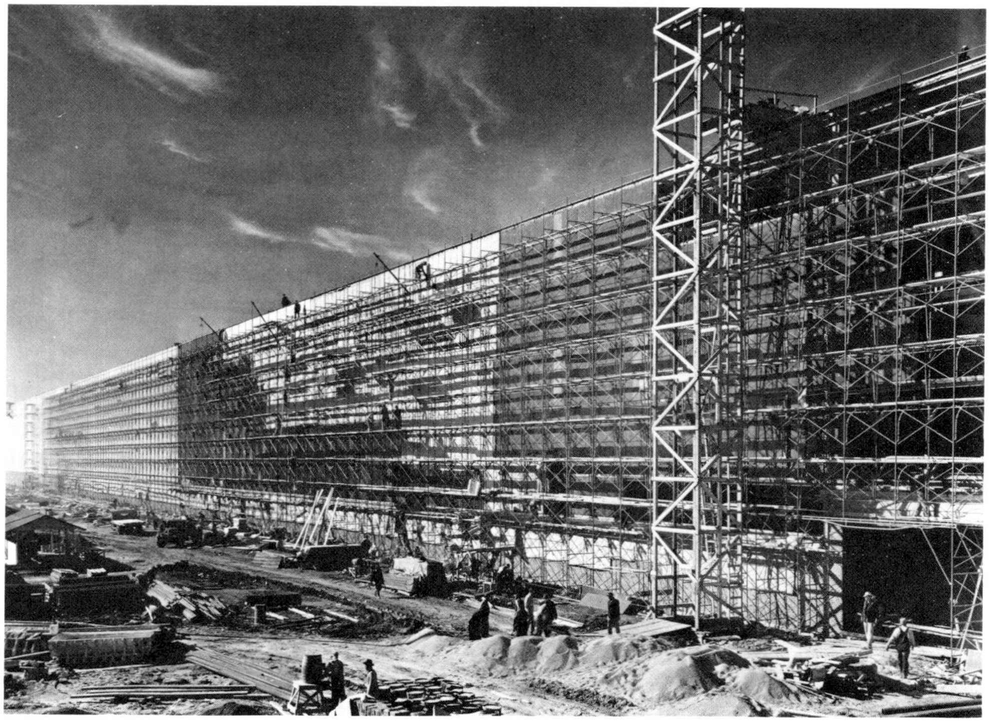

On the site of what is now Chicago's O'Hare Airport, Austin designed and constructed the world's largest all-timber factory building (1943) for the production of Douglas C-54 transport planes. *Above:* Unfurling the flag atop the final truss of the framework. *Left* and *below:* Despite wartime shortages, the company maintained its reputation for building handsome structures. Asbestos cement siding enclosed sidewalls of the Chicago plant, and continuous bands of wood ventilating sash outside the building columns gave the building its striking modern appearance.

Familiarity with the design of welded structures aided the speedy completion of plants for the production of magnesium, iodides, and many other chemicals. *Left:* One of the five wartime Dow Chemical Company plants (1943). A B-29 Superfortress is towed from the final assembly line at the Boeing plant in Wichita, Kansas (1944). *Below:* The Torpedo Attack Trainer (1943) at Quansit Point, Rhode Island, one of the developments of Austin's Special Devices Division.

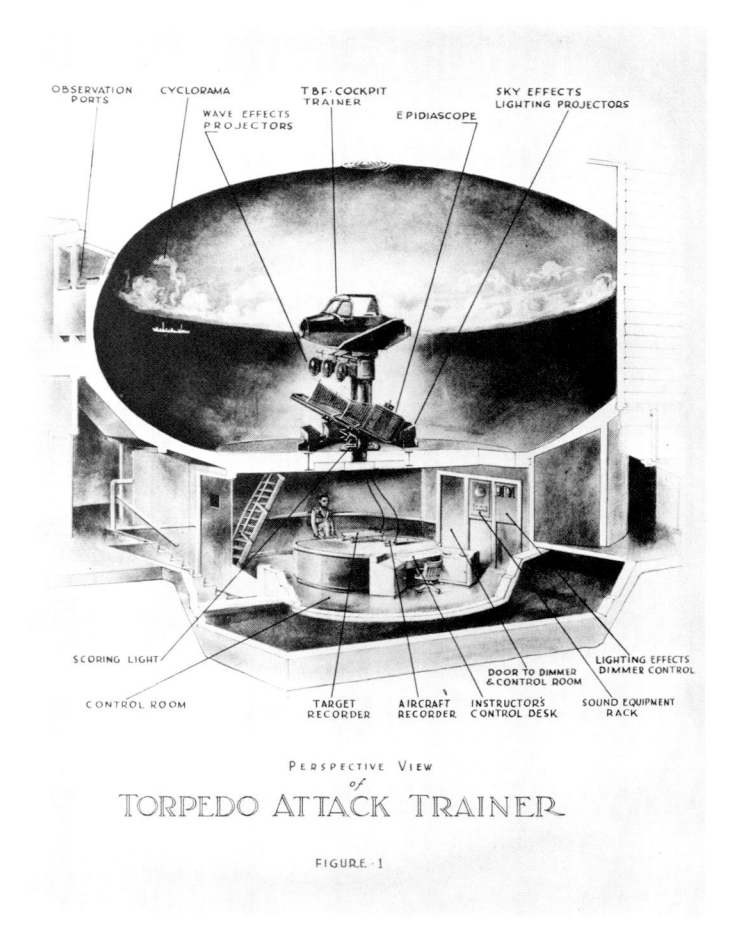

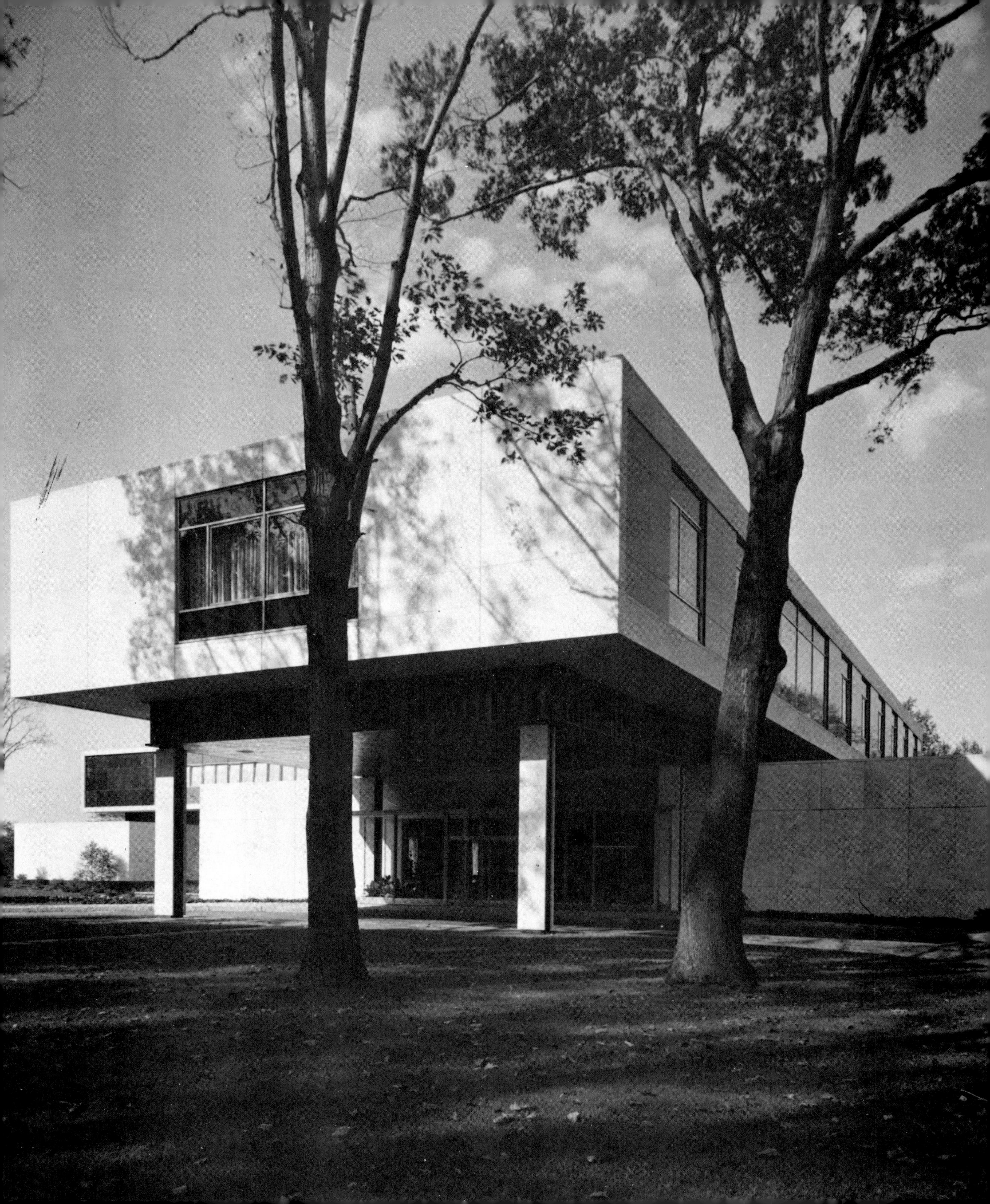

V An International Organization

The Postwar Era

On July 16, 1945, a month before World War II came to an end, the dawn came up like thunder at Alamogordo, New Mexico. "It was a sunrise such as the world had never seen," an observer wrote, "a great, green supersun, lighting up earth and sky with a dazzling luminosity." From a 100-foot tower the first atomic bomb had exploded with the power of 20,000 tons of TNT. As he watched the awesome blast, Dr. J. Robert Oppenheimer recalled a line of Hindu scripture: "Now I am become death, destroyer of worlds." A new chapter in twentieth-century history had begun, a chapter which by no means has yet been concluded.

When it comes to reviewing the events of the twentieth century, most commentators agree that there are three well-defined periods to be studied. Thus, in writing about economic history, for example, Peter Drucker can say with authority: "Twentieth-century history, up to the 1970s, can be divided into three major periods: the period before the outbreak of the First World War in 1914—a period culturally and politically much like the 19th century; the First World War and the twenty years from 1918 to the outbreak of World War II in 1939; and from World War II until today."

The trouble with this neat scheme, as generally correct as it might be, is that the further we move into the last quarter of the century, the larger and more unwieldly this third historical period becomes: The years "from World War II until today" now total the number of years in the first two periods combined. Another problem, of course, and one of an entirely different nature, is the difficulty of approaching the recent past with any reasonable degree of historical objectivity. We lack, in short, a true perspective of recent events. And we are burdened, as well, by a growing tendency to view the past *not* through the finely-polished lens of history, but through the carnival glass of nostalgia. The late '40s and early '50s witnessed a growing nostalgia for the '20s; the early '60s looked back with renewed regard for the '30s; almost everyone skipped the '40s; and now, with increasing intensity, a popular wave of nostalgia for the 1950s has set in. And the result, dismally evident on TV screens, is a distortion of events at best, a deliberate fabrication at worst. Most who lived through the 1950s, in fact, cannot imagine what there is to feel nostalgic about in the first place.

Opposite: General Offices, The Austin Company, Severance Center, Cleveland, Ohio, designed in 1959.

Some Generalizations

For many people, the first fifteen years after the war represented the best that America had to offer—usually expressed in material terms: television sets, hi-fis, two automobiles, a secure job with a large corporation, a house in the suburbs. Yet for others it seemed a less than idyllic time. Television constituted a vast "cultural wasteland"; hi-fis blared the gratingly raucous music of over-indulged youth; cars sported more horsepower, more chrome, and more lethal tail fins. The organization men preached rugged individualism, but practiced a rigid conformity, living in a suburbia of prefabricated boxes, each sprouting a TV antenna on the roof.

The cult of "conspicuous consumption" was the result of much of the nation achieving middle-class status following World War II. A booming economy, wartime savings, credit plans, and the urgings of Madison Avenue created a heady atmosphere for the generations of Americans that had suffered the economic frustrations of the Great Depression and the material sacrifices of the war. Tired of crises, the growing middle class sought only to return to the tasks of raising a family, making money, and living comfortably. Over millions of television sets the fatherly face of President Eisenhower smiled approvingly.

We are left, then, with a series of generalizations about the recent past that, for the moment, must suffice for another decade, as least. Whether or not they hold water the future will decide.

The Automobile and the New Industrial Landscape

Generalizations notwithstanding, there is at least one characteristic of the period that is indisputable: the dominance of the automobile in American life. Few technological developments, as almost everyone knows, have had more far-reaching social and economic consequences than the motor vehicle. It transformed transportation by land and changed the living habits of people throughout the world. Through the automobile the technique of mass production was finally worked out to create what, in effect, was a new industrial revolution. In the United States the manufacture of motor vehicles became the nation's largest industry, and automotive output became the prime index of the state of the economy. By its mere existence the motor vehicle created a need for innovations in highway design and construction and compelled efforts to meet that need; it expedited the movement of population from cities to suburbs, and by making people more mobile, it thereby uprooted them. It made itself economically indispensable and an integral part of modern culture, but it brought with it problems of traffic congestion and atmospheric pollution that most people learned to tolerate if they could only get home through the jammed highways to their air-conditioned split-level subdivisions.

The almost universal ownership of automobiles in America also made possible something else: the widespread adoption after the war of Austin's controlled conditions plant and of the single-story straight-line plant in general. The new horizontality of industrial design required large tracts of land, inexpensive land; and a mobile populace accelerated a process, already evident in the late '30s but interrupted by the war, of industry's migration from the cities to rural areas. The result is perhaps the most dynamic, visible characteristic of the postwar era—the creation of new suburbs in the middle of corn fields, the rise of supermarkets and vast shopping centers to meet the needs of the new communities, the proliferation of highways to reach the former corn fields, and the construction of still more industrial plants and corporate offices along the new highways as the corn-field suburbs grew to the size of small cities. This phenomenon is at the very heart of the new industrial landscape.

The extraordinary versatility of The Austin Company's work during this period reflects, of course, the continuing refinements of its engineering technology and the uninterrupted maintenance of its reputation for excellence and for speed. Even before the war it had developed ways and means to enhance the benefits of the controlled conditions plant while substantially reducing its cost, an effort that continued ceaselessly in other areas of research during the postwar period and kept the company well in advance of the myriad technological changes that seemed to make each morning's work obsolete by evening. One could consult the list of clients during this period—many, if not most, of the *Fortune* 500, and smaller firms that seemed to be reasonably certain candidates for future lists—and be suitably impressed by the success of the company that Samuel Austin founded. The sheer variety is staggering: newspaper plants, television studios (40 of America's first 100 stations), research laboratories, corporate offices, college dormitories and classrooms, hospitals, food processing plants, automated warehouses and supply centers, department stores—and on

Industry Moves to the Suburbs

and on and on. But little or none of this variety—and sheer volume—could have been possible without the dramatic socio-economic change taking place in the new America on wheels.

Industry Moves to the Suburbs

One can choose at random almost any Austin project of the period and discover the same story: the suburbanization of American industry. The story behind the design and construction of the Automatic Electric plant in Northlake, Illinois, is typical of hundreds of other projects undertaken by Austin. This mid-1950s structure is neither the largest nor the most important project of the period; it is simply typical—a paradigm of the postwar era.

A division of General Telephone Corporation, Automatic Electric was in the '50s the largest manufacturer of equipment for America's independent telephone companies. A burgeoning postwar economy made it necessary for General Telephone to centralize its manufacturing facilities that had grown so rapidly in the years following the war that it now occupied seventeen different buildings, comprising seventy-five floors, in downtown Chicago.

Plant Location

Realizing from the start that it would require consultation with plant location experts in the search for a suitable site, General Telephone commissioned The Austin Company to make a plant location survey, specifically requesting that Austin find out just what land might be available for this purpose in communities friendly to business nearest to the population center of the company's employees at that time.

At the same time Austin engineers were also authorized to make a comprehensive engineering survey and report through which Automatic Electric enlisted the benefit of their broad experience for the solution of plant layout and materials problems that would be encountered in the development of a completely new and integrated production concept.

This report established the minimum floor space needed to house efficiently all of the operations, and to provide for 100 percent expansion in manufacturing capacity from the very start. Though the Automatic Electric management had started out with 60 acres as the minimum requirement for any new plant site, Austin engineers pointed out that they might be inviting trouble if they had anything less than 100 acres. The fact that the aggregate floor space in the initial plant was increased by nearly 20 percent within a few months after construction started, bringing the total area under one roof to more than 35 acres, certainly confirmed Austin's judgment.

Studying the communities within a radius of 20 miles by census tracts to establish which communities would be the most likely to be a source of future manpower with the required skills and interests, The Austin Company turned up eleven available tracts with seven having definite possibilities. Austin engineers were investigating the details of each site with respect to utilities, local government set-up, long-range traffic outlook, and zoning problems, when they learned that one parcel, a 167-acre golf course at Northlake, was up for immediate sale. Austin's plant location staff quickly marshalled all the facts which they had been able to obtain on the various sites and proposed a definite course for immediate action.

They pointed out that the Northlake property, located on the Chicago & Northwestern Railroad adjacent to its huge North Proviso yards, appeared to have as many advantages, if not more, than any of the other sites under consideration. The availability of power, of a good water supply, and the general lay of the land from the standpoint of drainage were all in its favor, indicating that it would be an excellent piece of property for economical development.

The Triumph of the Straight-Line Plant

Eighteen months later, the 1,520,000 square foot integrated plant —the administrative complex of which had employed the then-radical lift-slab technique in its construction—was completed. The physical transfer of manufacturing operations, from a complex of 17 multi-story buildings near the Chicago Loop to an enormous single-story box-like structure sprawled over 35 acres of a one-time suburban golf course, permitted the arrangement of all handling, processing, storage, assembly, and shipping functions in an orderly, straight-line sequence. Now everything moved in more or less parallel lines from the receiving area on the north, to the finished stores, packing, and shipping departments on the south. With 7,200 manufacturing employees under one roof and members of the office, research, and administrative staff at work in modern office space directly adjacent to the factory, the Automatic Electric

Company achieved unity of operations in record time. But it also had a responsibility unique in the postwar era.

It now found itself guardian of its employees' automobiles. In addition to special parking areas for visitors and vendors directly adjacent to the separate executive office and purchasing department entrance, the plant had two large paved employee parking areas with accommodation for a total of 5,000 cars. Nearly three miles of blacktop and concrete roads had been installed to handle traffic in the 167-acre site.

Although this project has been selected at random from many hundreds of Austin projects, it serves nonetheless as an exemplar of the dominant trends of the postwar period. The golf course, for example, could easily have been an early industrialist's great estate or a once-profitable dairy farm, both of which, as the suburbs began to expand, could no longer afford the luxury of their valuable open space. And the plant could easily have been a shopping center or a laboratory or a computer center for a bank or for an insurance company. But the basic pattern is the same. Moreover, the paradigm is equally instructive of Austin's flexibility in dramatically changing times, providing as it does a convenient reinforcement of themes stressed earlier in this book. It graphically illustrates the vitality of the Austin Method in the postwar era. Essentially, the Automatic Electric plant reflects the fundamental principle of "undivided responsibility" established by the Austins —father and son—at the beginning of the century and in no way changed over the years. It has simply evolved to match the times. As modern technology has become more and more sophisticated, Austin's range of services has expanded to mirror all the latest technological developments. The range of services may have been narrower in 1911 or 1912 than they were in the mid-50s, just as they are even broader today at the company's centennial. But the essential credo of the Method—"from planning to production"— remains constant.

When the Automatic Electric Company's integrated plant was dedicated, the headline in one Chicago newspaper was revealing, if not prophetic: DOWNTOWN UNITS CENTRALIZED IN SUBURBS. The headline, in fact, is a capsule history of postwar industrial design itself.

A Worldwide Technological Civilization

A second and altogether different sort of generalization that can be made about the postwar era is its distinct international flavor—the world is definitely smaller than it was before the war. The two-way exchange of worldwide culture is easily demonstrable. It is reflected in virtually every aspect of American life—even the most trivial—from BankAmericard's change of name to the less provincial "Visa" to the almost faddist cultivation of European and Oriental gourmet cooking and the sudden transformation of Americans into tipplers of imported wines. We, in turn have drowned the rest of the world in Coke, fed the multitude on Big Macs, and spread the gospel of rock 'n' roll in all its decibels, so that a trip abroad, spent at a Holiday Inn, is free from the last vestiges of "foreignness" that once characterized international travel.

History, of course, will have to confirm this generalization, but the most important effect of World War II seems readily apparent. It brought modern technology in its most advanced forms directly to the most remote corners of the earth—and established a worldwide technological civilization.

Given this more serious consequence of contemporary internationalism, it is hardly surprising that the postwar period witnessed The Austin Company's gradual—and conservatively cautious—development into an international organization.

Austin Abroad Austin had, of course, been an international presence since the introduction of its standard factory buildings in 1914. These early prefabricated structures had been exported for erection in places as far away as South Africa, Turkey, Greece, and Bulgaria. And Wilbert Austin's trip to Europe in 1918, immediately after the armistice, led to the company's first truly international project: the reconstruction of Belgian glass plants destroyed in the war.[1] The 1930s saw a number of international projects—from the establishment of a Canadian branch office in 1930 and the construction of the Molotov plant at Gorki, to the design of airplane manufacturing plants for the Republic of China in 1933 and the inauguration of Austin's first European office five years later.

---

[1] Wilbert Austin's diary of his trip abroad in 1918 has been preserved. It is a warm and richly humorous account of the difficulties encountered by "an American in Paris" attempting to do business with French industrialists after a six-day cram course in *le Français*.

The events surrounding Austin's establishment of its first European office in London in 1938 are indicative of its serious commitment to international development as long as forty years ago—in spite of the raging worldwide Depression. Surviving correspondence proves that George Bryant was eager to enter into further dealings with the Russians and believed that American assistance of such "underdeveloped" nations as Russia was not only good for business, but would in the long run prove beneficial to humanity in general. But the real prime mover in expanding the company abroad was young Allan S. Austin, who at twenty-five had worked on the Russian project and, at thirty, succeeded in opening the company's first office in London.

The London office had come about indirectly—through advertisements in *Fortune*. The management of an English-organization, Smith's Delivery Vehicles, aware of Austin through its advertisements, wrote directly to *Fortune* for information about the Cleveland company. The inquiry led to a substantial contract—and to a base and time schedule that gave Allan Austin the opportunity of establishing a European branch office once that project had been completed. Although its brief existence brought into being one of Austin's handsomest buildings of the '30s—the British Technicolour laboratory—the office was forced to close at the outbreak of World War II the following year.

Austin International   If Samuel Austin established the company and developed it into a major *local* contracting firm, and Wilbert Austin oversaw its growth as a *nationwide* organization, then Allan Austin—during his presidency—fulfilled a long-standing dream by expanding its services *internationally*. The company began working in South America shortly after World War II, and it established a subsidiary in Brazil in 1955. In 1960 the global arm of the company, Austin International, was founded, and subsidiaries were simultaneously established in Great Britain, France, and Australia. Since that time, and during the administrations of Austin's successors, Harold A. Anderson and Charles A. Shirk, other Austin offices have been opened in Argentina, Belgium, Canada, Germany, Greece, the Netherlands, Italy, Japan, and Spain.

Each of these subsidiaries is a completely integrated and autonomous operating unit, fully staffed for administrative, sales, and technical functions. Like its American district counterparts, each has a permanent complement of planners, architectural designers, engineers, estimators, purchasing agents, accountants, construction supervisors, and field personnel. And it is perhaps no exaggeration to say that in recent years some of Austin's most impressive work has come out of its international offices.

A Century of Results

By 1980, a single electronics complex in Sidi-bel-Abbes, Algeria, will provide enough television sets, radios, stereos, cassette players, and related entertainment products to meet the needs of the entire country. The technologically sophisticated complex will cover an area of one million square feet, and will be uniquely self-sufficient—producing not only the finished consumer goods, but most of the components that go into them.

The Austin Company will engineer and build the manufacturing plant and, in addition, will design and construct a complete workers' village, consisting of 77 houses, 65 apartments, a commercial shopping center, and recreational facilities, including tennis courts, swimming pools, and soccer fields.

While the project is expected to fulfill a great need by providing Algeria with a communication and entertainment products plant, it will have other significant benefits. The facility will bring a new technology to Algeria, train people in a sophisticated area of electronics, and provide thousands of new jobs.

Thus, as it enters its second hundred years, The Austin Company finds itself for the first time in its history on the continent that very possibly holds the key to the future of civilization as we know it today. Its work in Algeria demonstrates the power of advanced technology to make possible systematic economic development through industrialism—and raises the promise of what President John F. Kennedy once called "the rising tide of human expectations," the hope that technology can banish the age-old curse of disease and early death, of grinding poverty, and ceaseless toil. In its century of results, The Austin Company has helped to accomplish these goals in America. Now it is participating in the achievement of this aim in a worldwide technological civilization.

What better birthday present could the heirs of the carpenter from Orton Waterville ask for?

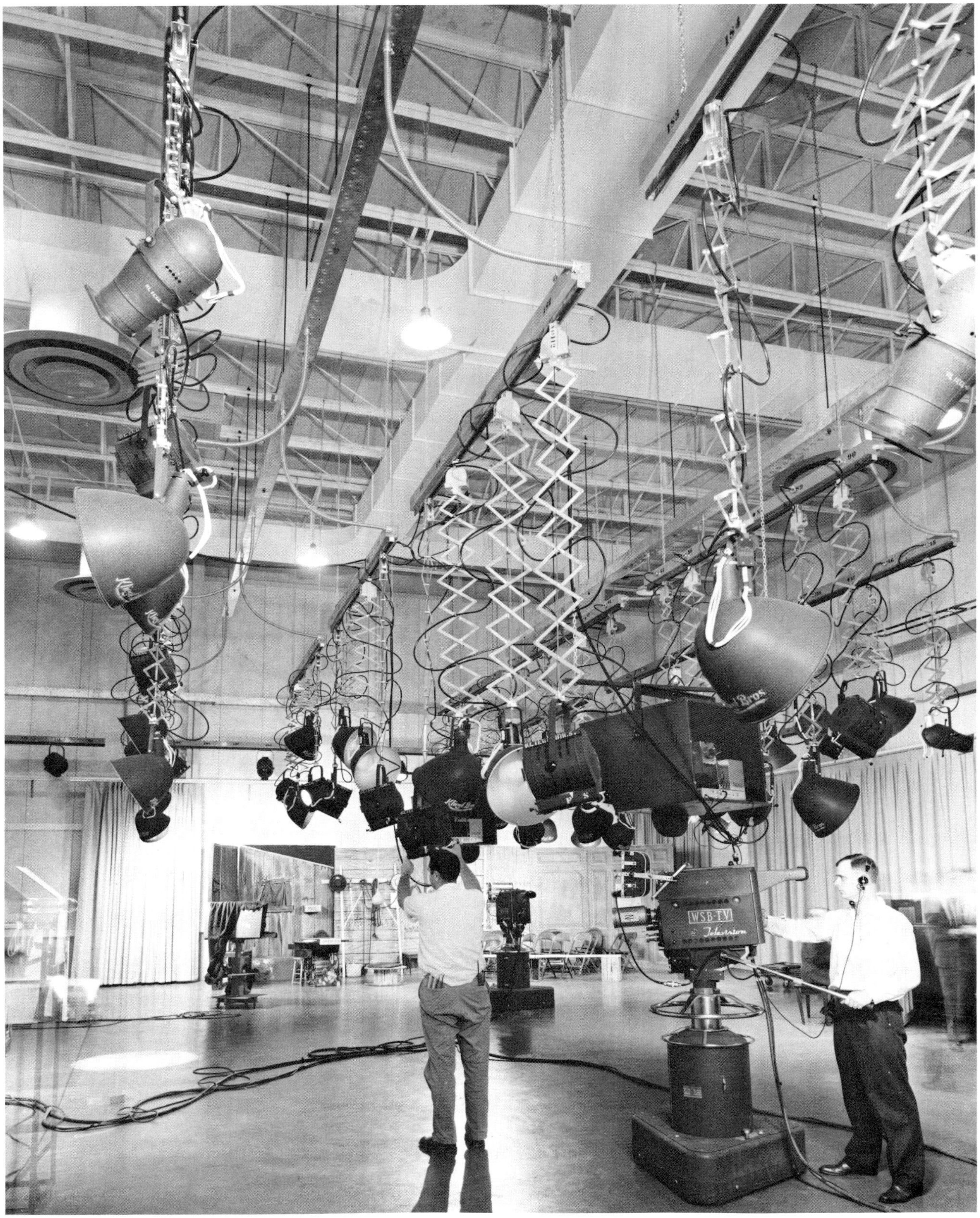
WSB-TV

Austin established its lead in the design and construction of television studios during the immediate postwar years, maintained it in the development of some of the nation's earliest color television facilities, and epitomized its lead in constructing the superb CBC Broadcasting Centre at Montreal's Expo '67. *Opposite:* WSB studio, Atlanta, Georgia (1954). *Above:* WCAU, Philadelphia, Pennsylvania (1952). *Right:* ABC-TV studios, Hollywood, California (1961).

Industry's postwar move to the suburbs led to landscaped campus-like settings, an innovation anticipated in part in 1913 by General Electric's Nela Park, actively advocated by Austin throughout the '20s and '30s, and almost universally adopted from the late '40s on. *Below:* Phillips Laboratories, Briarcliff Manor, New York (1964). *Opposite:* Automatic Electric Company, Northlake, Illinois (1955); Research Laboratory, Motorola, Inc., Riverside, California (1954).

155

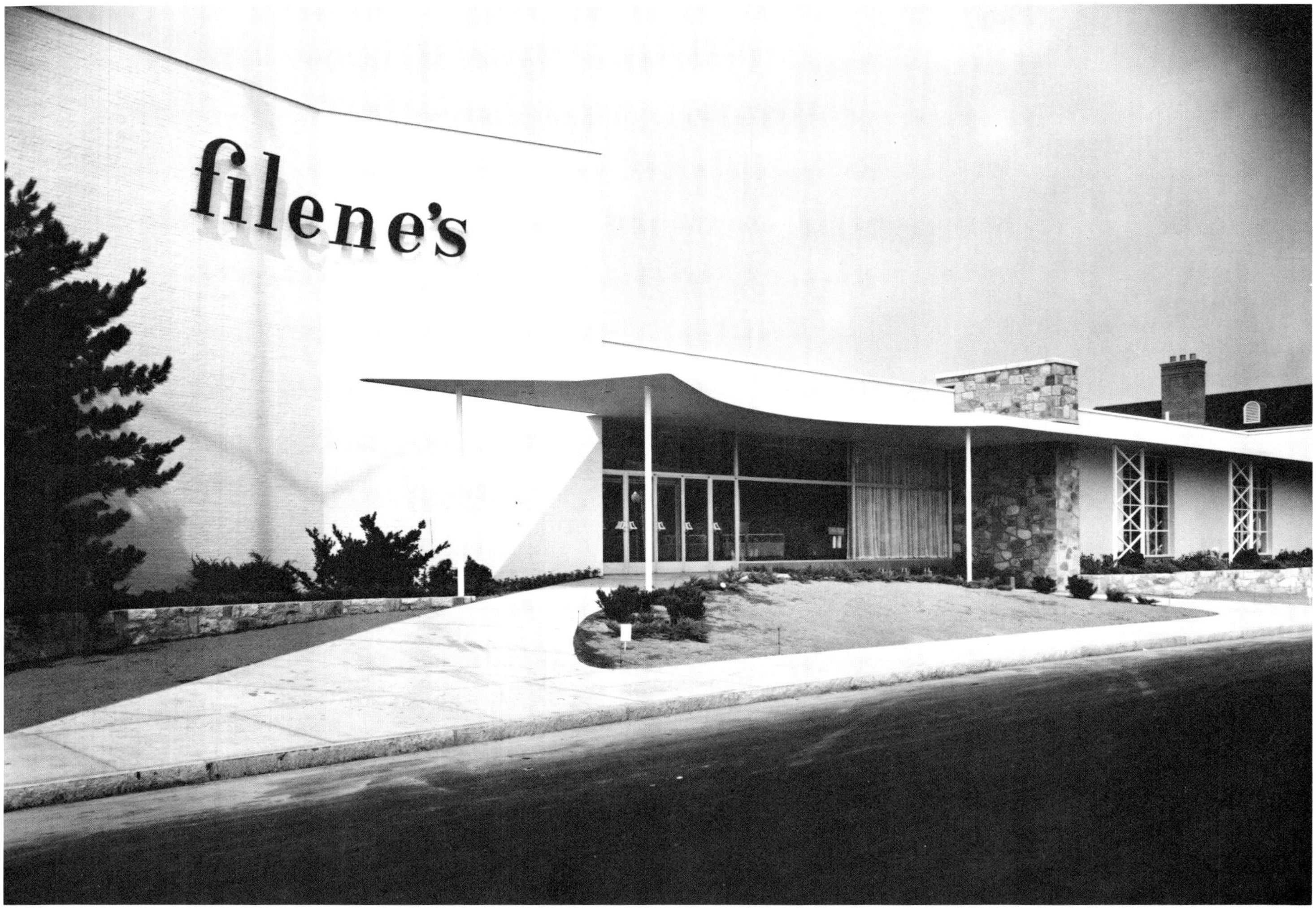
filene's

The move of industry to the suburbs necessitated the development by urban department stores of suburban branches and the eventual construction of massive shopping centers and malls. *Opposite* and *below:* Two early postwar suburban department stores. Filene's, Chestnut Hill (Newton), Massachusetts (1949); Bloomingdale's, Stamford, Connecticut (1952).

Right: Main Laboratory Building, Eastern Research Center, Stauffer Chemical Company, Chauncey, New York (1964). *Below:* Machining plant, Chrysler Corporation, Perrysburg, Ohio (1966). *Opposite:* The first major Japanese plant in the United States, for Kikkoman Shoyu Co., Ltd., producers of soy and teriyaki sauce, and located—after an Austin study—in the heart of soybean and wheat country, Walworth County, Wisconsin (1971); the computer-controlled Food Processing Center, Kitchens of Sara Lee, Inc., New Hampton, Iowa (1971).

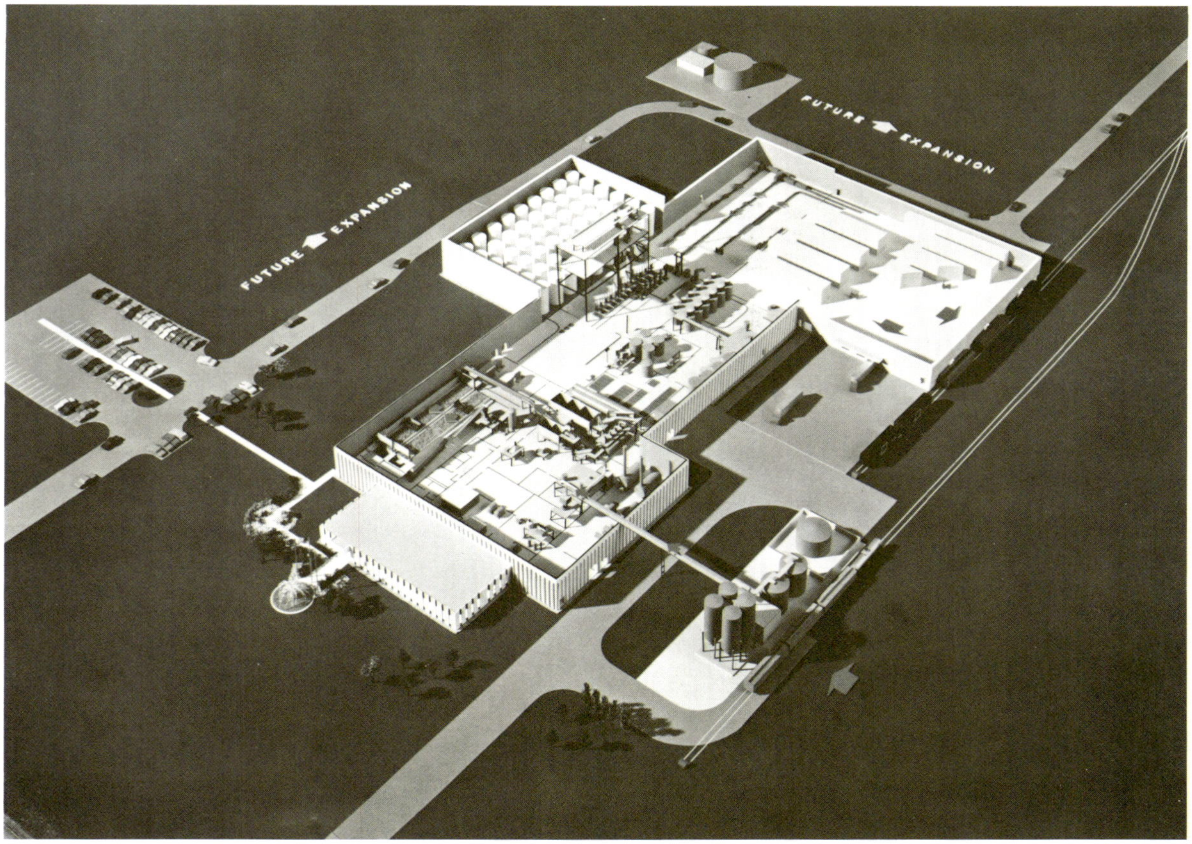
FUTURE EXPANSION
FUTURE EXPANSION

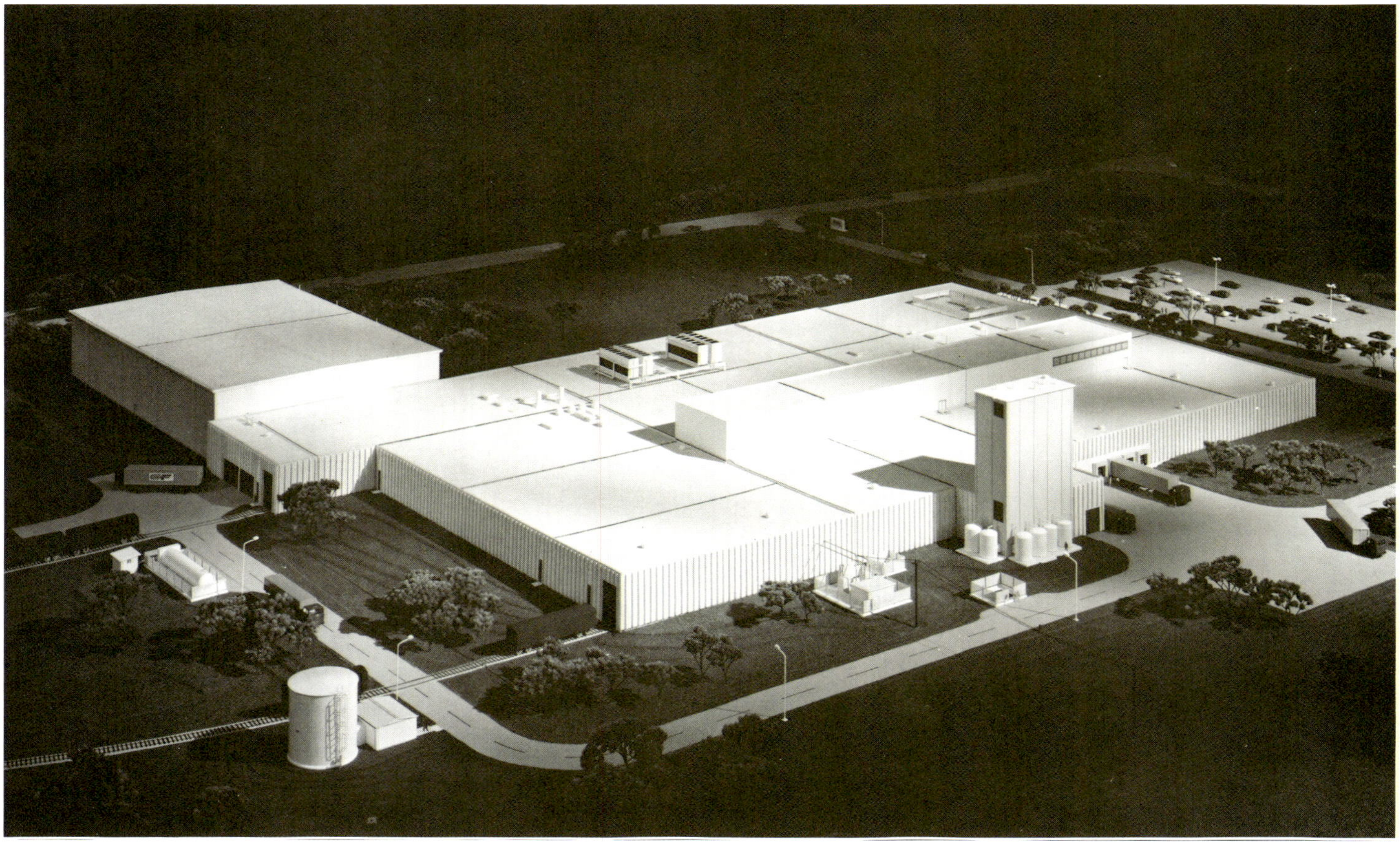

Some of the most interesting aspects of Austin's work are to be found in the field of special purpose facilities. *Above:* Space environment chamber, Boeing Space Center, Kent, Washington (1965); antennae for the Austin-built Voice of America, Greenville, North Carolina (1962). *Right:* The test at Austin's Bliss Mill that led America into the age of prestressed concrete industrial building (1951).

Below: The Austin Spira-Park, an innovative attempt at solving one of the postwar era's most pressing urban problems (1964). In 1951, Austin designed at Idaho Falls the first experimental breeder reactor and also the first nuclear reactor which produced usable electrical energy. EBR-1, just one of Austin's early nuclear energy projects, became a registered historic landmark in 1966.

Magnesium Production Plant, Dow Chemical Company, Freeport, Texas, 1959.

Pasta Plant, Barilla S. p. A., Parma, Italy, 1968.

Corporate Headquarters, Abello, S. A., Madrid, Spain, 1972.

Corporate Offices, General Electric Plastics, Evry, France, 1975.

Corporate Headquarters and Research Laboratory, Oakite Products, Inc., Berkeley Heights, New Jersey, 1966.

Administration Building, Standard Electrica S. A., Madrid, Spain, 1970.

Corporate Research Center, Ling-Temco-Vought, Inc., Grand Prairie, Texas, 1967.

Technical Center, The Clorox Company, Pleasanton, California, 1971.

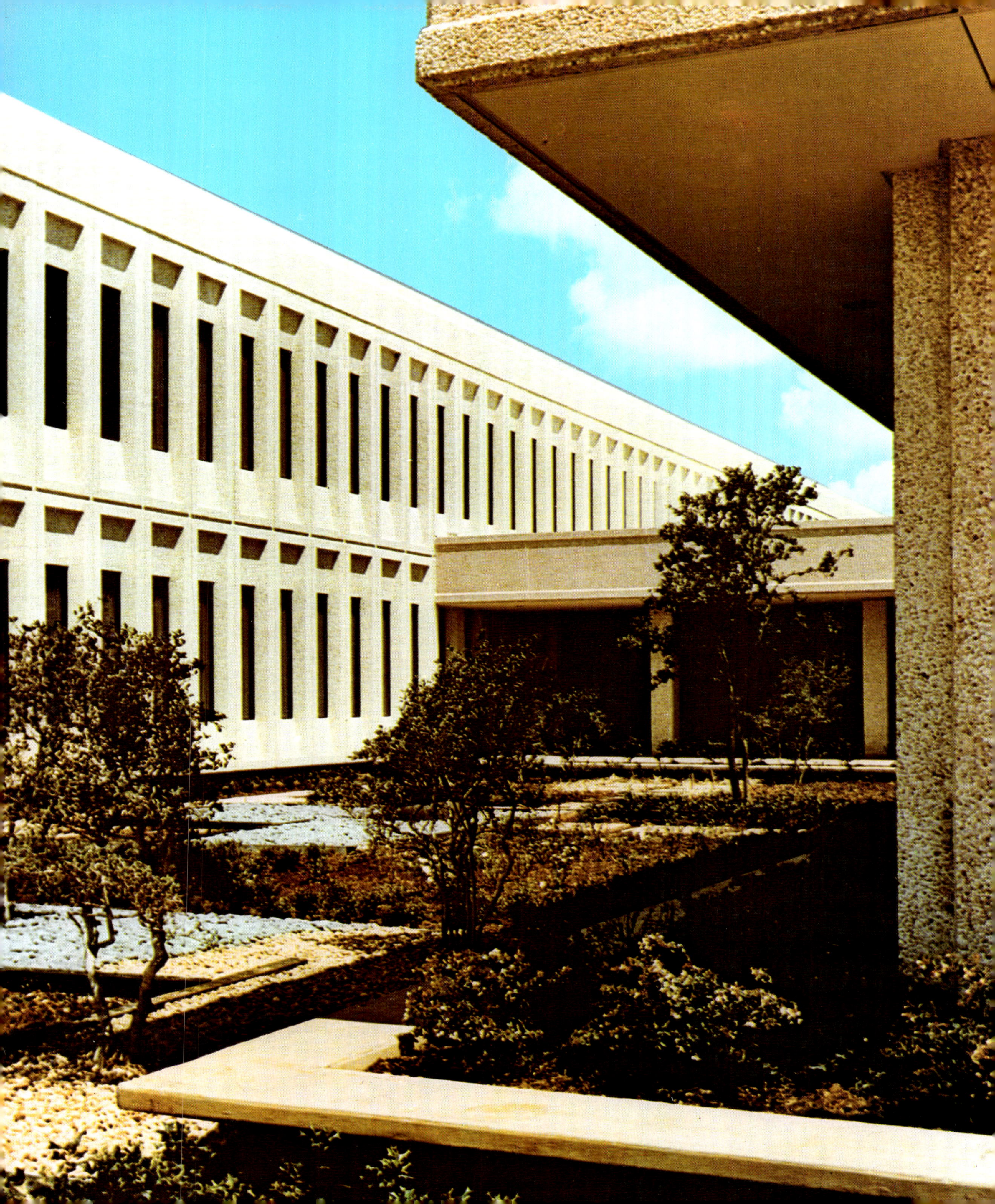

Imax Theater, Cedar Point, Inc., Sandusky, Ohio, 1975.

Technical Center, The Clorox Company, Pleasanton, California, 1971.

Rifamycin Facilities, Lepitit, S. p. A., Brindisi, Italy, 1970.

Cafeteria, Merlin-Gerin, Grenoble, France, 1970.

Conex Division Administration Building, Illinois Tool Works, Des Plaines, Illinois, 1961.

Computer Center, The Firestone Tire & Rubber Company, Akron, Ohio, 1967.

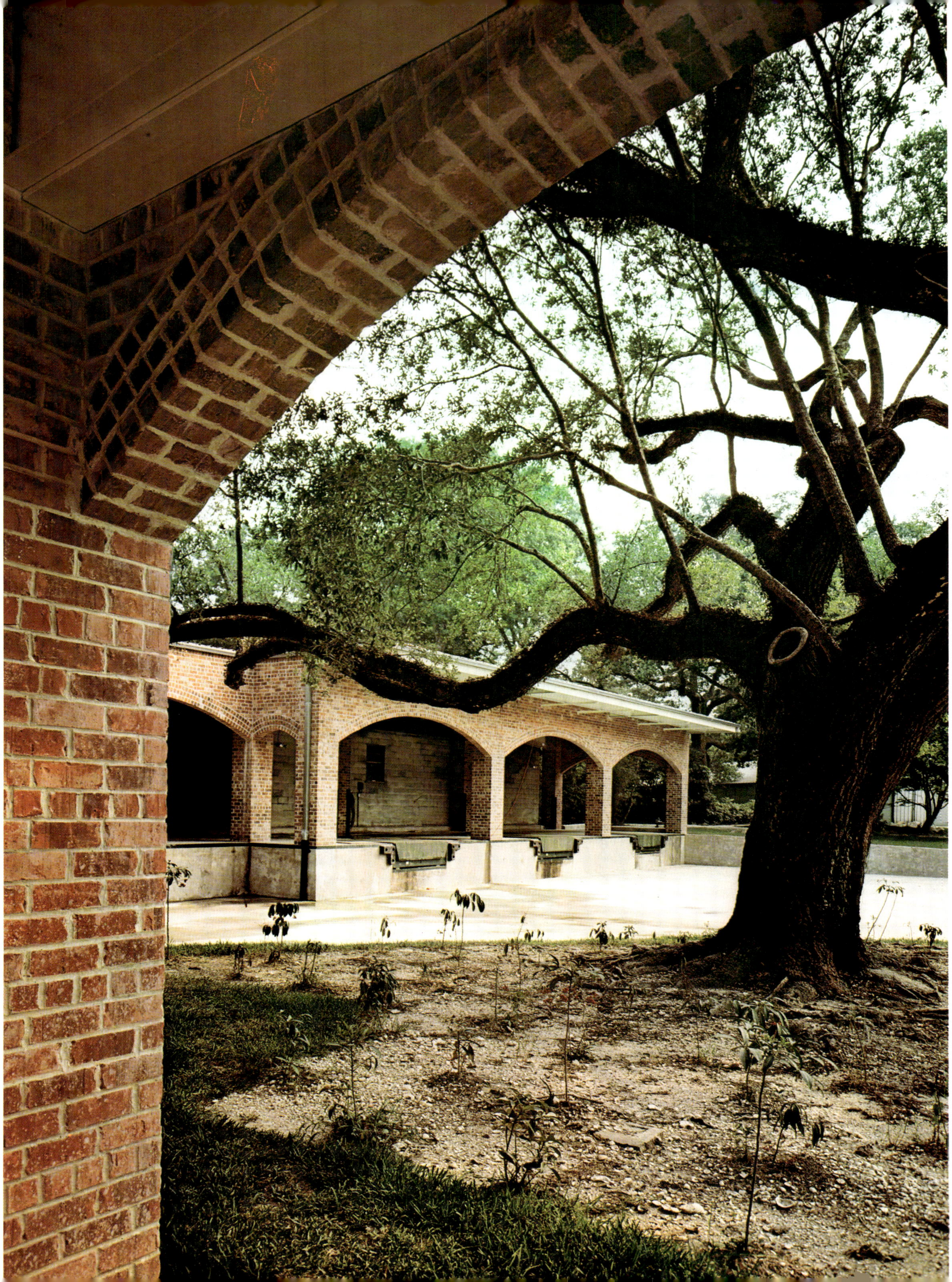

Dormitories, Case Western Reserve University, Cleveland, Ohio, 1967.

Warehousing Facilities, McIlhenny Company, Avery Island, Louisiana, 1971.

Electronic Data Processing Center, Ohio National Bank of Columbus, Columbus, Ohio, 1971.

Bon Marché, Inc., Baton Rouge, Louisiana, 1974.

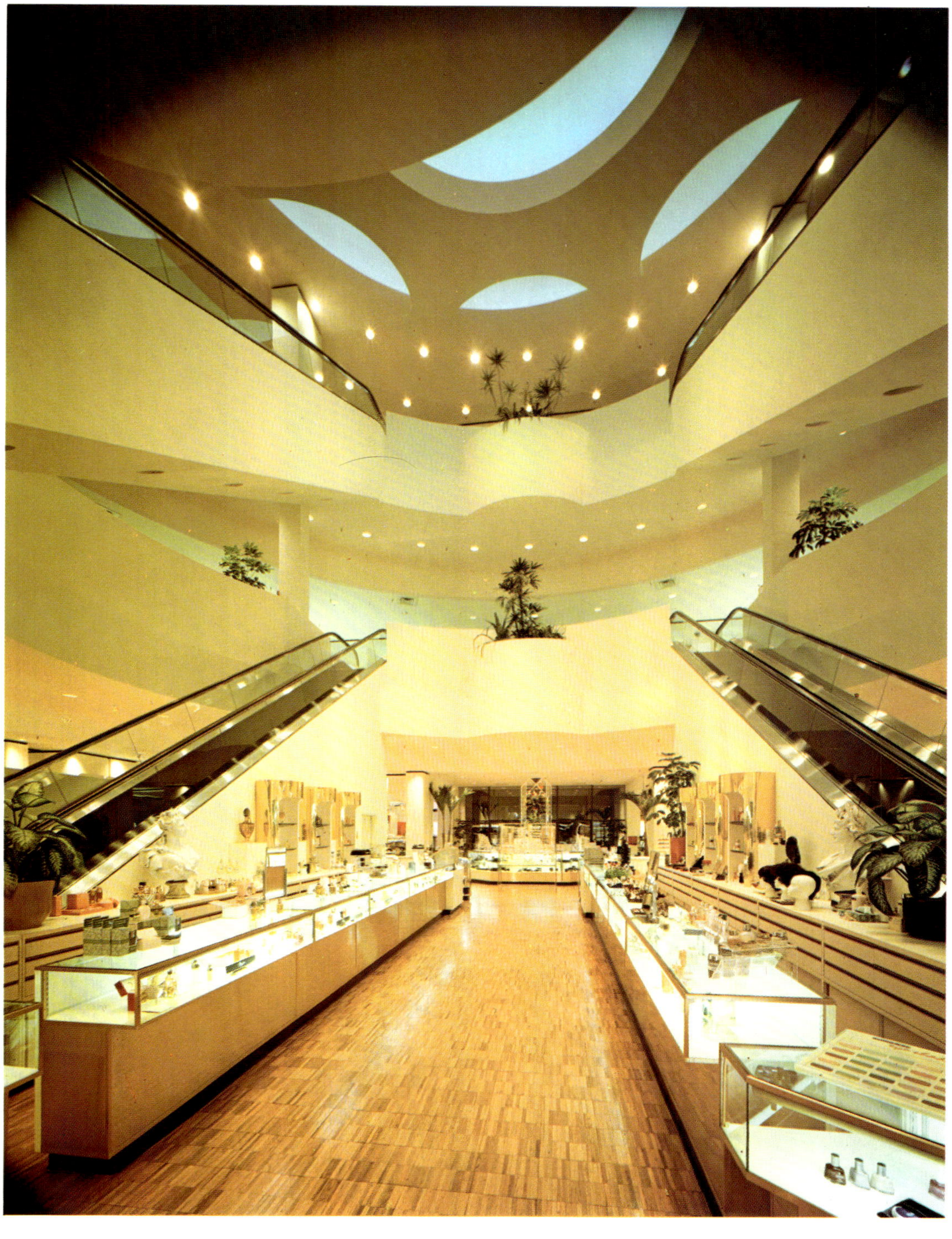

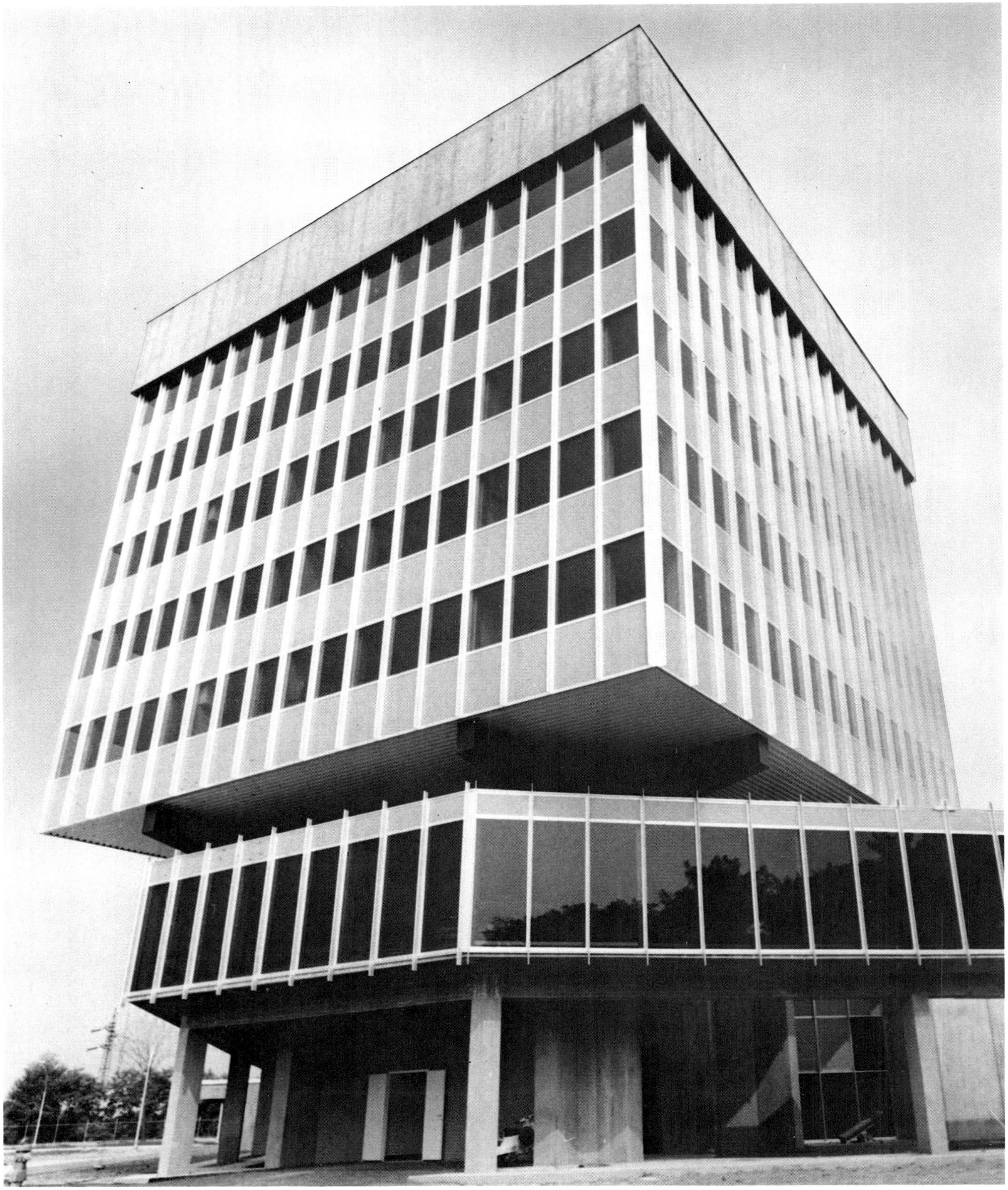

Opposite: Headquarters and Distribution Center, S. C. Johnson & Son Italiana, Arese, Italy (1971). *Right:* Electronic Data Processing Center, Grumman Aircraft Engineering Corporation, Bethpage, New York (1966). *Below:* Corporate Technical and Services Center, Hooker Chemical Corporation, Grand Island, New York (1968).

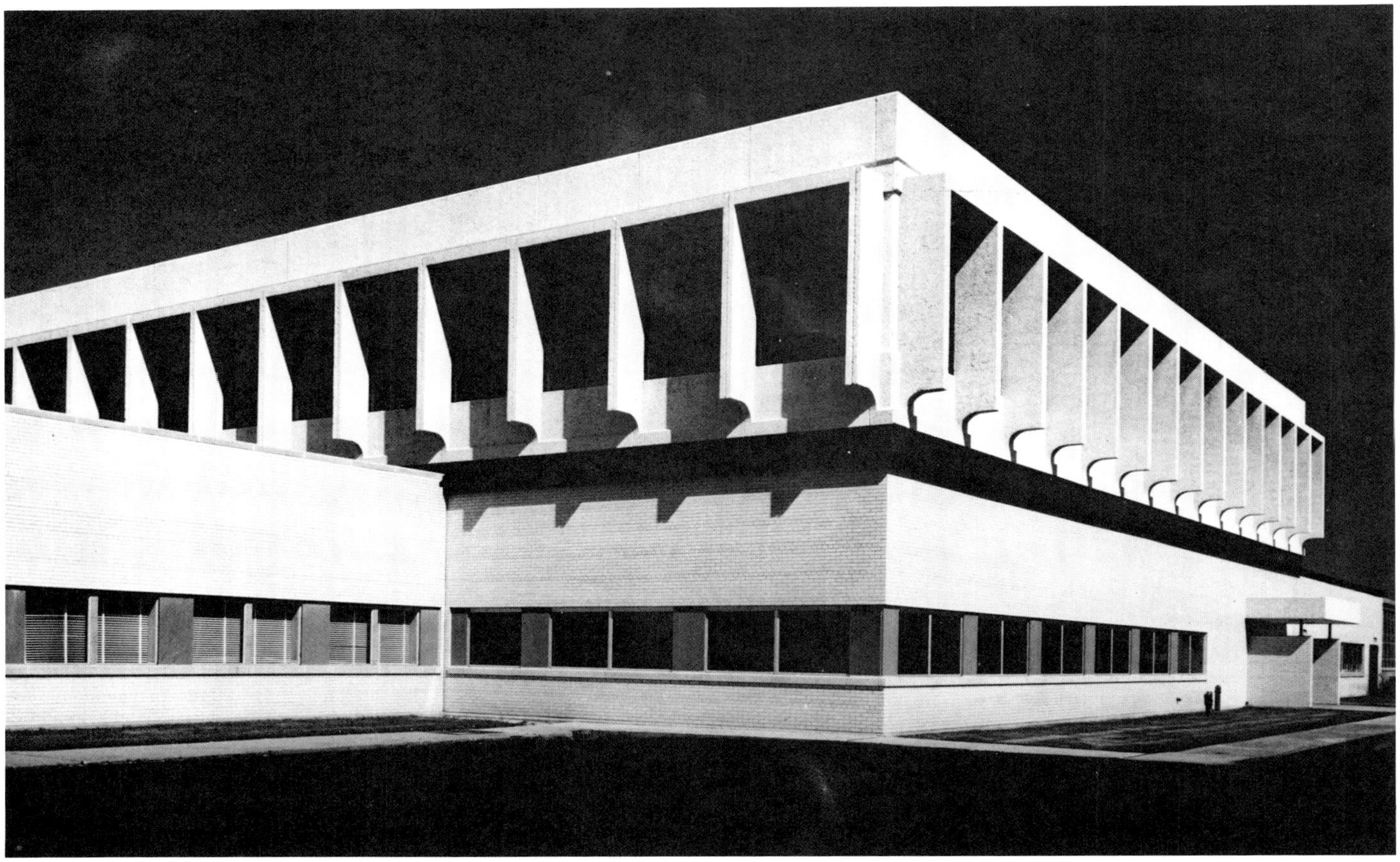

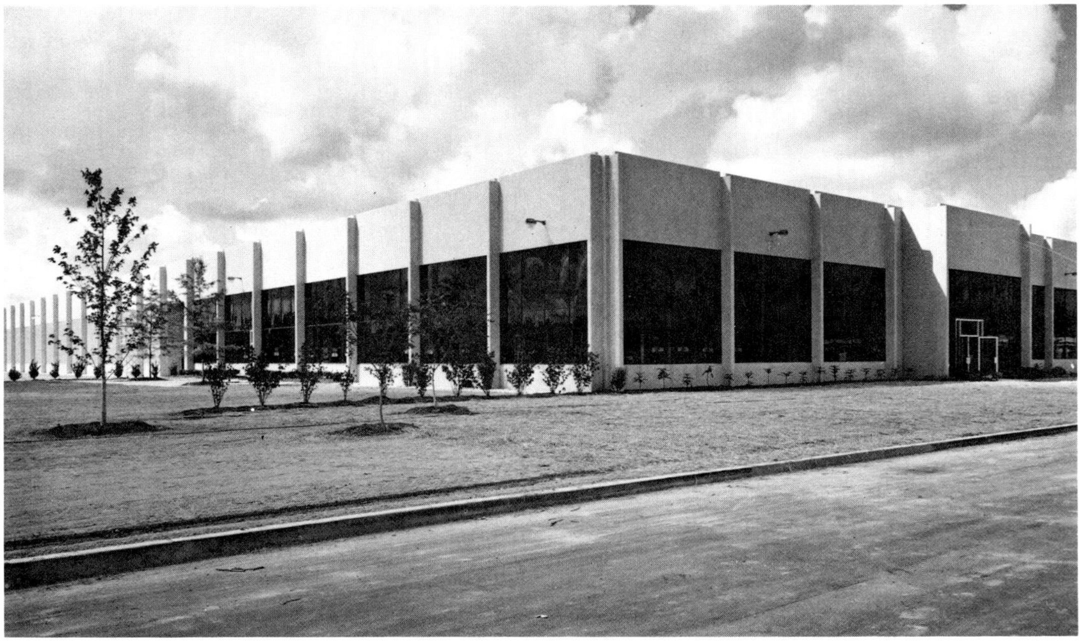

Opposite (above): Food Administrative Offices, Crane Packing Company, Morton Grove, Illinois (1971). *Opposite (below)*: Production Plant, Lufkin Rule Company, Apex, North Carolina (1967). *Above:* Pharmaceutical Plant, Lepetit, S.p.A., Alcala de Henares, Spain (1969–70).

Kettering Hall, Oberlin College, Oberlin, Ohio, 1961.

VI The Second Hundred Years

In 1849, a year before Samuel Austin was born, his fellow countryman John Ruskin wrote that "there are only two fine arts possible to the human race: sculpture and painting. What we call architecture is only the association of these in noble masses, or the placing them in fit places. All architecture other than this is, in fact, mere *building*." Ruskin was neither disparaging function at the expense of ornamentation, as some modern interpreters have maintained, nor hastening a fatal split between the professions of architecture and engineering. Ruskin was simply reminding high-minded Victorians that most "architecture"—far from being the "mother of the arts"—was in actuality no more or less than the noble and ancient craft of building. Two years later, at the completion of Paxton's glass and iron Crystal Palace, he wrote that "we require from buildings, as from men, two kinds of goodness: first, doing their practical duty well; then that they be graceful and pleasing in doing it." Utility and Beauty were obviously two sides of the same Ruskinian coin.

In 1910, six years after the incorporation of The Samuel Austin & Son Company, the Viennese architect Adolf Loos, who modestly but proudly insisted upon calling himself a "builder," wrote that "only a small part of architecture has anything to do with art: the tomb and the monument. Everything else, everything which is built for functional purposes, must be excluded from the concept of art." Within a few years of this grimly witty statement, Albert Kahn, who built virtually all the Ford Motor Company facilities in its pioneering days, was to pronounce what critic Ada Louise Huxtable only recently called a "notorious dictum." "Architecture," he said, "is 90 percent business and 10 percent art." Mrs. Huxtable's opinion to the contrary, the architect's deep-felt observation was made not merely to please "his businessmen clients," but was born of the firm knowledge, presumably unfathomable to critics, that, for every structure ever built since the dawn of economic man, someone has had to foot the bill—most frequently, in fact, the oft-maligned "businessmen" whose capital is rarely if ever credited for having established the architectural movement we now so proudly proclaim as "modern."

Most contemporary critics, ignoring industrial architecture in general and eschewing building as a means of production in particular, have much to learn from the thoughtful humility of Ruskin and Loos and Kahn. They might profitably contemplate instead of "art," the keen observation of Friedrich Semper, a noted nineteenth-century German architect. Upon seeing Paxton's Crystal Palace for the first time, Semper declared prophetically that "architecture, above all else, must come down from its throne and go into the market place to teach there, as well as to learn." And by "the market place," he meant specifically the new world of industry, knowing at first hand what popular history has now forgotten: Paxton's immense iron and glass structure—a veritable palace of industry—developed logically from its simple function. It was designed to house an exhibition of raw materials, machinery, manufactures, and mechanical invention—a display called *not* The Great Exhibition of 1851 as textbooks have prosaically embalmed it, but The Great Exhibition of the Industry of All Civilised Nations of the World. Intended to assemble under one roof the entire panorama of Victorian industrial art, it was a machine-age building for a new industrial age.

Within the vastness of its glass-walled nave and transept, its avenues and halls, technology was idolized—some six million people having visited the industrial shrine in its first five months to gape in wonderment at the miraculous new machines. Four years later, across the sea, the poet Whitman would be invoking the lacy strength of structural iron, "Singing the great achievements of the present,/ Singing the strong light works of engineers," a hymn of affirmation to the inventive genius of sentient man. The nineteenth century, if it was nothing else, was the age of invention—the age of Edison, Bell, Marconi—the age of the inventor who acted alone on sudden inspiration, apparently accidental, which somehow provided the germ of invention.

And then, in 1879, Edison "invented" innovation: To solve the filament problem of the incandescent lamp necessitated scientific teamwork, hitherto unknown, which in its germinal form soon evolved into the system of technological work—organized research—and the development, early in the twentieth century, of such corporate research laboratories as Nela Park. The end of such organized research is innovation: technology used as a means of effecting change in the economy, in society, in culture—in short, in the life of the average man.

Innovation begets innovation. It is hardly accidental that the efficiency of the Austin Method was first measured against the mass production of the incandescent bulb or that it evolved still further through extensive building for the automotive industry in the early years of this century. The tungsten filament was an innovation. The Model T was an innovation. The single-story standard factory building was an innovation. Nela Park was an innovation. Each one in its own way increased the influence of technology and its impact on the way people live. Edison, Ford, and Kahn were innovators all, the very warp and woof of industrial technology whose separate strands, so inextricably woven in the social and economic fabric of America, have formed the repeating patterns of this book. And the Austins were innovators, too.

Samuel and Wilbert Austin—a father and son in whom the nineteenth and twentieth centuries met—contributed no important technological *invention*. The creation of the Austin Method, as they designed and perfected it between 1901 and 1914, contained not a single new element: the carpenter-builder had been responsible for most of the design and construction in America at least two centuries before the Austin Method of Undivided Responsibility was conceived; standardization of design had been a reality since the adoption of uniform design for watchmen's shanties and other small railroad buildings; stocking of building materials had been a long-established practice of many contractors; prefabricated cast-iron beams and columns had been employed by James Bogardus two years before Samuel Austin was even born. But the contribution of the Austins was nonetheless a dynamic *innovation*, a technical solution to the economic problem of how to produce a variety of efficient industrial buildings with the greatest reliability of quality and safety in the shortest period of time and at the lowest possible cost. Responsible during the company's first hundred years for the completion of more than twelve-thousand facilities for general manufacturing, food production, chemical processing, banking and electronic data processing, warehousing and distribution, offices, research and development, communications, institutions, health care, mining, metals processing, cement production, and retail merchandising, the Austin Method has touched consequently on virtually every aspect of modern life—from a flight aboard a 747, or the computerized printing of the daily newspaper, to the packaging and distribution of the cereal on this morning's

The Cleveland Health Museum and Education Center, Cleveland, Ohio, 1971.

Corporate Offices and Technical Center, General Electric Plastics, Evry, France, 1975.

WCPO-TV, Scripps-Howard Broadcasting Company, Cincinnati, Ohio, 1967.

breakfast table: from the wondrous to the mundane. This single innovation has more than likely had a greater impact on the way we live than many of the technical inventions of the past.

During the past fifteen years, a period in which science fiction has been rendered real, the technical community has witnessed an unparalleled growth in technological development. Frontiers, not simply broken, have been shattered. New production techniques, methods, and equipment have given way and whole technological eras ended. Yesterday's simple electro-mechanical devices now employ optics and lasers for measurement and digital servos for precision positioning—all controlled by micro-computers. Simple problems and simple solutions are simply no more.

But the Austin Method, the bedrock of the company's first hundred years, will see it well into its second, having anticipated not only the problems of a rapidly changing technology, but a means toward their eventual solution as well. For the Austin Method anticipated systems engineering, itself a logical extension of innovation and a conception now being widely acclaimed as one effective problem-solving technique in a vast array of twenty-first-century fields ranging from space exploration to atomic and solar energy to urban congestion. The road ahead is surely rocky—the energy crisis is only just beginning, technology itself is under popular attack, and the Austin Method has attracted more imitators than the company cares to count—but no one really questions the inevitable. So long as its code of business ethics remains inviolable and it continues to supply the increasingly sophisticated building and consulting needs of its clients, The Austin Company will leave its imprint on the international industrial landscape of the future.

In the lobby of The Austin Company's corporate headquarters, and directly beneath the office of its president—the first of a new generation that knew neither Samuel nor Wilbert Austin—stands a stately grandfather's clock, eight feet tall at least, and weighing nearly half a ton. Its case is hand-carved of the finest English walnut, and its face and works reflect the centuries-old heritage of British craftsmanship. This was Samuel Austin's clock, and it is the one material embodiment of the man that survives on the premises today. Before this monumental timepiece pass daily the engineers and architects, the employees, who, in accordance with his wishes, will eventually own all the shares in the company that bears his name. The building in which the clock stands is functional yet simple, elegant and undated, despite its conception in the late '50s, perhaps the darkest days of American design. It is a structure in which the permanence, dignity, and quality of the materials used reflect the integrity, stability, and progressiveness of the company itself, and a triumph of unornamented architecture that would have won the praise of the "builder" Adolf Loos.

Within this setting of artless architecture, the fine old stately clock stands comfortably at home. One cannot forget, after all, that the word architecture, *in its simplest Greek origins, once meant "the work of the master carpenter." Samuel Austin, had he known, would have been pleased.*

Division Office Building, Safeco Insurance Company of America, Cincinnati, Ohio, 1970.

Index

Abello, S.A. (Madrid, Spain), *164*
Acme Stores (Akron, Ohio), *122*
Adams Bag Company (Chagrin Falls, Ohio), *40*
Advanced Technology Systems, *132–33*
Advertising, *59, 61–64, 94, 103, 104*
Airport design, *88, 89*
All-Steel-Equip Company (Aurora, Illinois), *121*
American Broadcasting Company (Hollywood, California), *154*
American Rolling Mills (Middletown, Ohio), *121*
Antrol Laboratories, Inc. (Los Angeles, California), *123*
Apartment houses, *42, 86*
Anderson, Harold A., *103, 150*
Architectural form, *23* ff., *103* ff.
Army-Navy "E", *132*
Art Deco style, *104, 110–11*
Art Nouveau style, *38*
Austin, Allan S., *98* n, *150*
Austin, Ida Stewart, *30*
Austin, Mary, *25, 27, 29*
Austin, Samuel, *10, 15, 18, 23, 24, 31, 33, 34, 37, 38, 53, 61, 64, 145, 181, 183, 186–87*
  birth: *25*
  apprenticeship: *25–26*
  autobiography: *25–34*
  emigration: *26–27*
  marriage: *28*
  establishment as entrepreneur: *28* ff.
  first shop: *30* ff.
  character: *32* ff.
  early buildings: *33* ff.
  The Samuel Austin & Son Company, incorporation of: *34* ff.
  The Austin Company, change of name to: *59–60*
  appearance in World War I advertisement: *62*
  inception of employee-ownership plan: *66*
  retirement: *66*
  death: *105*
Austin, Sara Gynn, *27, 28*
Austin, Thomas, *25, 26, 29*
Austin Wilbert J., *24, 28, 30, 34, 35, 57, 58, 60, 67, 88, 130–31, 132, 149, 150, 183, 186;* Engineering Building (Cleveland, Ohio), *104–05, 120, 131*
Austingrad. *See* Autostroy
Austin Method, *18, 34* ff., *37, 60, 61, 65, 66, 95, 148, 183, 186*
Automatic Electric Company (Northlake, Illinois), *146–48, 156*
Automobile and American life, *144* ff.
Automotive industry, *56, 65, 78, 79, 183*
Autostroy, *97–102, 106–07*
Aviation, *13–15, 60, 61–62, 67, 72, 73, 88–89, 122, 128, 129* ff., *134–43, 145, 160, 177*

Banks, *19, 33, 34, 38, 174*
Barilla S.p.A. (Parma, Italy), *163*
BASF-Wyandotte Corporation (Geismar, Louisiana), *22*
Bell Aircraft Corporation (Niagara Falls, New York), *134*
Black, H., Co. (Cleveland, Ohio), *40*
Bliss Mill (Cleveland, Ohio), *59, 61, 160*
Bloomingdale's (Stamford, Connecticut), *157*
Boeing Aircraft Company: (Renton, Washington), *21;* (Seattle, Washington), *122, 134, 135;* (Wichita, Kansas), *141;* Boeing 747 assembly plant (Everett, Washington), *13–15;* Boeing Space Center (Kent, Washington), *160*
Bogardus, James, *183*
Bon Marché, Inc. (Baton Rouge, Louisiana), *175*
"Breathing" walls, *131, 136, 138*
Broadway Savings Bank (Cleveland, Ohio), *33, 34*
Bryant, George A., *94, 99, 103, 105, 107, 132, 150*
Buckeye Electric Company (Cleveland, Ohio), *33, 56*

Cadillac Motor Car Co. (Detroit, Michigan), *82*
Canadian Broadcasting Corporation, *153*
Canfield Oil Company (Cleveland, Ohio), *33*
Cantilever hangars, *67, 88*
Cape Town [South Africa] Explosives Company, *74*

189

Carnegie Medical Building (Cleveland, Ohio), 110
Carpenter-builder, tradition of, 35, 183
Case Institute of Technology (Cleveland, Ohio), 34, 130
Case Western Reserve University (Cleveland, Ohio), 173
Caterpillar Tractor Co. (Peoria, Illinois), 81
Central Falls [Rhode Island] Lamp Works, 45
Cheasty's Department Store (Seattle, Washington), 84
Chicago Century of Progress Exposition, 111
Chicago fire, 26, 27
Chrysler Corporation (Perrysburg, Ohio), 158
Church and Dwight Company, Inc. (Syracuse, New York), 104, 115, 125
Clear-span steel truss, 68, 79
Cleveland [Ohio] Airport, 88, 110
Cleveland Health Museum and Education Center, 184
Cleveland Metal Products Co., 41
Clorox Company (Pleasanton, California), 166, 169
Color, industrial, 14, 97
Concrete: prestressed, 132, 160; reinforced, 18, 40, 123
Consolidated-Vultee (Fort Worth, Texas), 131, 138–139
Controlled conditions plants, 95–97, 104, 129 ff., 136–139, 145
Coolidge, Calvin, 66, 102
Coulton's Store (Cleveland, Ohio), 40
Crane Packing Company (Morton Grove, Illinois), 173
Creamer/FSR, Inc., 63
Crown Zellerbach Corporation (Camas, Washington), 123
Crystal Palace, 25, 181, 182
Curtiss Aeroplane & Motor Corporation (Buffalo, New York), 61–62, 72

Depression Modern style, 103 ff., 112–117, 120–27
Depressions. *See* Panics
Dippel, Henry, 31, 33
Dirigible hangers, 89
Dominion Chain Co. (Niagara Falls, Ontario), 75
Dominion Glass Co. (Redcliff, Alberta), 75
Dominion Steel Products Co. (Brantford, Ontario), 74

Douglas Aircraft Co., Inc.: (Chicago, Illinois), 128, 132, 140; (Oklahoma City, Oklahoma), 131, 136–37; (Tulsa, Oklahoma), 131
Dow Chemical Company, 141, 162
Drive-in facilities, 78, 103, 116–17, 122
Drucker, Peter, 143
Du Bois Press (Rochester, New York), 83

Edison, Thomas Alva, 182, 183
Electro-Motive Corporation (La Grange, Illinois), 2
Engineering surveys, 146–47
Erdman store (Cleveland, Ohio), 33
Experimental breeder reactor [EBR-1] (Idaho Falls, Idaho), 168
Expo '67, 153

Filene's (Newton, Massachusetts), 156
Firestone Tire & Rubber Company (Akron, Ohio), 171
First Security Corporation (Salt Lake City, Utah), 19
Five-Year Plan, First, 97
Fluorescent lighting, 104, 129–30, 131, 136, 138
Ford, Henry, 58, 97, 98, 183
Ford Motor Company, 98, 99, 181
Fortune magazine, 9, 63, 94, 95, 104, 113, 118–19, 145, 150
Frankford Arsenal (Philadelphia, Pennsylvania), 60–61, 72
Fuller & Smith & Ross. *See* Creamer/FSR, Inc.

Gair Company (Piermont, New York), 52
Gannett, J. K., 129
Garages, 69, 79, 167
General Electric Company, 33, 36, 154; (Evry, France), 164, 184
General Motors Corporation, 98, 129
General Motors Sales Corp. (Phoenix, Arizona), 124
German American Portland Cement Works (La Salle, Illinois), 52
Goodyear Tire and Rubber Co. Pavillion (Century of Progress), 111
Goodyear Zeppelin Corporation (Wheeling, West Virginia; Round Hill, Massachusetts), 89
Grumman Aircraft Engineering Corp. (Bethpage, New York), 130, 177

Hangar design, 67, 88
Hills Bros. Coffee, Inc. (Edgewater, New Jersey), 120

Hooker Chemical Corporation (Grand Island, New York), *172*
Hoover, Herbert, *93–94*
Huxtable, Ada Louise, *181*

Illinois Tool Works (Des Plaines, Illinois), *171*
Imax Theater (Sandusky, Ohio), *168*
Incandescent lamp industry, *34, 36 ff., 39, 43, 44–45, 56, 57, 95, 183*
Industrialism, history of, *16 ff.*
Industrial research centers, *46–47, 182*
Innovation, nature of, *95 ff., 182 ff.*
Internationalism, *149 ff.*
Invention, age of, *16 ff., 55, 182*

Jefferson Apartments (Cleveland, Ohio), *42*
Johnson Motor Co. (Waukegan, Illinois), *81*
Johnson, S. C., & Son, Italiana (Arese, Italy), *176*

Kahn, Albert, *9, 181, 182, 183*
Keck, George Fred, *9*
Kikkoman Shoyu Co., Ltd. (Walworth, Wisconsin), *159*
Kitchens of Sara Lee, Inc. (New Hampton, Iowa), *20, 159*
Kress, S. H., & Co. (Tacoma, Washington), *84*

Laundries, *65, 83*
Lepetit S.p.A.: (Alcala de Henares, Spain), *175*; (Brindisi, Italy), *170*
Lescaze, William, *9, 126*
Ling-Temco-Vought, Inc. (Grand Prairie, Texas), *167*
Link-Belt Co. (San Francisco, California), *81*
Literary Digest, *59, 61, 62*
Logotype, Austin, *35, 67, 103*
Loos, Adolf, *181, 182, 187*
Lower Carnegie Building (Cleveland, Ohio), *91, 95*
Lufkin Rule Company (Apex, North Carolina), *178*

McIlhenny Company (Avery Island, Louisiana), *172*
Magnesium production, *141, 162*
Mars Incorporated (Chicago, Illinois), *87*
Mendelsohn, Erich, *18*
Mentor Harbor [Ohio] Yacht Club, *82*
Merlin-Gerin (Grenoble, France), *170*
Merlini, Pedro, S.A. (Buenos Aires, Argentina), *75*

Mildred Apartments (Beaumont, Texas), *86*
Models. *See* Prototype models
Monsanto Company (Bath, Ohio), *22*
Motorola, Inc. (Riverside, California), *155*

National Advisory Committee for Aeronautics (Langley Field, Virginia), *88*
National Broadcasting Company (Hollywood, California), *92, 104, 120, 126–27*
National Cash Register Company (Dayton, Ohio), *70–71*
National Electric Lamp Association, *36, 44*
National Lamp Works (Oakland, California), *44*
National Reactor Testing Station (Idaho Falls, Idaho), *168*
Nation's Business, *119*
Nela Park (Cleveland, Ohio), *36–37, 46–47, 56, 154, 182, 183*
Nelite plant (Cleveland, Ohio), *36–37, 56*
Niles [Ohio] Glass Works, *39*
Nizhni Novgorod (U.S.S.R.). *See* Autostroy
North American Philips (Briarcliff Manor, New York), *154*
Nu-Art Engraving Co. (Chicago, Illinois), *85*

Oakite Products, Inc. (Berkeley Heights, New Jersey), *165*
Oakland Motor Car Co. (Pontiac, Michigan), *78, 79*
Oberlin [Ohio] College, *180*
Offices, district, *59, 60*; international, *149 ff.*
Ohio Bell Telephone Co. (Cleveland, Ohio), *82*
Ohio Lamp Works (Warren, Ohio), *45*
Ohio National Bank of Columbus, *174*

Palmer House Hotel Laundry (Chicago, Illinois), *83*
Panics, economic: 1866: *26*; 1873: *28 ff., 85*; 1907: *35 ff.*; 1929–1939: *93 ff., 102 ff.*
Paxton, Joseph, *14, 25, 181, 182*
Pennsylvania R.R. (Logansport, Indiana), *76–77*
People's Mutual Building (Beverly Hills, California), *111*
Pittsburgh [Pennsylvania] Transformer Company, *95*

Plant location surveys, 146–47
Precision Spring Corp. (Detroit, Michigan), 124
Prefabrication, 61, 103, 183
Projects, variety of, 23, 65–66, 145–46, 183, 186
Prototype models, 104, 112–15, 119

Radio industry, 120
Railway industrial buildings, 64–65, 76–77
Residences, 42, 87
Richardson, C. E., 32
Rigid frame design, 104
Rollings, William, 25–26
Ruskin, John, 181, 182
Russian Ford plant. *See* Autostroy
Ryan, R. A., Motor Co. (Miami, Florida), 78

Safeco Insurance Company of America (Cincinnati, Ohio), 188
Saturday Evening Post, 59, 61, 62, 63, 70
Schaffer Training School (Cleveland, Ohio), 33
Scientific Management, theory of, 18
Scoon, Robert, 98 n
Scripps-Howard Broadcasting Company (Cincinnati, Ohio), 185
Sennett Film Corporation (Hollywood, California), 54, 80
Service stations, 78, 103 ff., 116–17
Sesquicentennial Exposition (Philadelphia, Pennsylvania), 91
Shirk, Charles A., 11, 150
Simonds, Gifford K., 96, 97, 129
Simonds Saw and Steel Company (Fitchburg, Massachusetts), 96–97, 104
Single-story industrial buildings, 95, 145, 183
Smith, Robert, Jr., 103
Sound stages, 54, 80, 131
South Cleveland [Ohio] Banking Company, 33, 38
Spanish Mission style, 86–87
Special Devices Division. *See* Advanced Technology Systems
Speed, Austin's reputation for, 58–59, 61, 70–71
Spira-Park, 167
Stalin, Joseph, 95, 97, 98, 102
Standard Daylight Factory Buildings, 57 ff., 68–69, 95, 183
Standard Electrica S.A. (Madrid, Spain), 165

Standardization, 55–59, 65, 95, 183
Standard railway buildings, 65, 76–77
Stauffer Chemical Company (Chauncey, New York), 158
Steel, fabrication of, 58–59, 60, 95
"Steelspan" buildings, 69, 79
Stewart, William B., 30–31
Stone, Edward Durell, 9
Straight-line plants, 145, 147
Suburban development, 145 ff., 154–59

Taylor, Frederick Winslow, 18
Teague, Walter Dorwin, 125
Technology, history of, 15 ff., 23, 55 ff., 182 ff., 186
Television studios, 133, 145, 152–53
Timber construction, 60, 132
Timken Roller Bearing Company (Canton, Ohio), 20
Torbenson Gear and Axle Co. (Cleveland, Ohio), 80
Torpedo Attack Trainer, 141
Troyan block (Cleveland, Ohio), 33

United Airport (Burbank, California), 68
United States Navy: Aircraft factory (Philadelphia, Pennsylvania), 61, 73; Bureau of Aeronautics, 132; Radio towers (Annapolis, Maryland), 61, 73
Upjohn Company (Kalamazoo, Michigan), 2

Vining, J., 28, 29
Voice of America (Greenville, North Carolina), 160

Wallace & Goodwillie, 46
WCAU (Philadelphia, Pennsylvania), 153
WCPO-TV (Cincinnati, Ohio), 185
Welding, 90–91, 95–96
Western Mineral Wool Company (Cleveland and Chicago), 33
Westminster College (New Wilmington, Pennsylvania), 19
Whitman, Walt, 182
Wind tunnels, 88, 131, 135
Wooltex Cloak factory (Cleveland, Ohio), 40
World War I, 17, 60 ff., 72–73, 149
World War II, 105, 128–141
Wright, Russel, 104
WSB (Atlanta, Georgia), 152

Youngstown [Ohio] Mazda Lamp Co., 43